D0926626

# AVERTING CATASTROPHE

# AVERTING CATASTROPHE

*Decision Theory for COVID-19, Climate Change, and Potential Disasters of All Kinds*

Cass R. Sunstein

NEW YORK UNIVERSITY PRESS

*New York*

NEW YORK UNIVERSITY PRESS
New York
www.nyupress.org

References to Internet websites (URLs) were accurate at the time of writing.
Neither the author nor New York University Press is responsible for URLs
that may have expired or changed since the manuscript was prepared.

Library of Congress Cataloging-in-Publication Data
Names: Sunstein, Cass R., author.
Title: Averting catastrophe : decision theory for COVID-19, climate change,
and potential disasters of all kinds / Cass R. Sunstein.
Description: New York : New York University Press, [2021] |
Includes bibliographical references and index.
Identifiers: LCCN 2020049518 | ISBN 9781479808489 (hardback) |
ISBN 9781479808502 (ebook) | ISBN 9781479808496 (ebook other)
Subjects: LCSH: Public administration—Decision making. |
Crisis management in government. | Emergency management.
Classification: LCC JF1525.D4 S86 2021 | DDC 352.3/301—dc23
LC record available at https://lccn.loc.gov/2020049518

New York University Press books are printed on acid-free paper, and their
binding materials are chosen for strength and durability. We strive to
use environmentally responsible suppliers and materials to the
greatest extent possible in publishing our books.

Manufactured in the United States of America

10 9 8 7 6 5 4 3 2 1

Also available as an ebook

By "uncertain" knowledge, let me explain, I do not mean merely to distinguish what is known for certain from what is only probable. The game of roulette is not subject, in this sense, to uncertainty; nor is the prospect of a Victory bond being drawn. Or, again, the expectation of life is only slightly uncertain. Even the weather is only moderately uncertain. The sense in which I am using the term is that in which the prospect of a European war is uncertain, or the price of copper and the rate of interest twenty years hence, or the obsolescence of a new invention, or the position of private wealth-owners in the social system in 1970. About these matters there is no scientific basis on which to form any calculable probability whatever. We simply do not know.
—John Maynard Keynes[1]


Uncertainty must be taken in a sense radically distinct from the familiar notion of Risk, from which it has never been properly separated. . . . The essential fact is that "risk" means in some cases a quantity susceptible of measurement, while at other times it is something distinctly not of this character; and there are far-reaching and crucial differences in the bearings of the phenomena depending on which of the two is really present and operating.
—Frank Knight[2]

In some cases, the level of scientific uncertainty may be so large that you can only present discrete alternative scenarios without assessing the relative likelihood of each scenario quantitatively. For instance, in assessing the potential outcomes of an environmental effect, there may be a limited number of scientific studies with strongly divergent results. In such cases, you might present results from a range of plausible scenarios, together with any available information that might help in qualitatively determining which scenario is most likely to occur.

—OMB Circular A-4[3]

# CONTENTS

Introduction   1

1. What We Don't Know   7

2. With and Without Numbers   16

3. The Maximin Principle   28

4. The Precautionary Principle   43

5. Uncertainty   61

6. Objections   72

7. Irreversibility   82

Conclusion   107

*Acknowledgments*   119

*Appendix A: Memorandum for the Heads of Executive Departments and Agencies*   121

*Appendix B: Circular A-4*   127

*Notes*   137

*Index*   157

*About the Author*   167

# Introduction

This book has an unusual origin. Under President Barack Obama, I served as Administrator of the White House Office of Information and Regulatory Affairs, which oversees federal regulation in domains that include highway safety, health care, clean water, air travel, agriculture, occupational health, homeland security, clean air, and climate change. One of our tasks was to help develop a "social cost of carbon"—a number that reflects the economic damage of a ton of carbon emissions.

This was, and is, an exceedingly important number. Among other things, it helps determine the stringency of regulations designed to control greenhouse gas emissions from motor vehicles and power plants. It is fundamental to climate change policy. Working on the social cost of carbon, to produce a concrete number, may have been the most difficult task of my professional life. It was difficult in part because of the known unknowns, and the unknown unknowns, and the challenge of deciding how to handle them. In some respects, we were flying blind.

Dozens of people were involved; many of them were experts on science, economics, or both. They disagreed on fundamental issues. They disagreed vigorously about the magnitude of the harmful effects of greenhouse gas emissions. They disagreed about how much was known and how much was unknown. They disagreed about how to handle the possibility of catastrophe and whether to build in a large margin of error, which would produce a much higher number. We were able to reach agreement, but it took many months, and (to put it gently) not everyone who joined the agreement thought that the resulting number was the best choice.

My aim here is to connect some important questions in regulatory policy with some fundamental issues in decision theory. We have many illuminating treatments of regulatory policy, often focusing on social welfare, cost-benefit analysis, and distributive justice. We have a great deal of illuminating work in decision theory, focusing on risk and uncertainty, and also on how people actually handle challenging questions. Most of the time, those who focus on regulation do not engage decision theory, and vice versa. If we bring the two together, we should be able to make some progress in handling some of the most difficult problems of the current era, including those raised by pandemics, climate change, and others that we can only glimpse (and perhaps not even that).

My main goal is to explore how to think about averting catastrophe, understood as extreme downsides, making human life immeasurably worse. But we should also attend to the possibility of miracles, understood as extreme upsides, making human life immeasurably better. In reducing the risk of the former, we should try our best not to reduce the possibility of the latter.

Consider in this regard a passage from John Maynard Keynes, who lived through the Great Depression and World

War II, who spent much of his young adulthood in same-sex relationships before he fell head over heels in love with a woman, and who knew a great deal about the unforeseeable:[1]

> By "uncertain" knowledge, let me explain, I do not mean merely to distinguish what is known for certain from what is only probable. The game of roulette is not subject, in this sense, to uncertainty; nor is the prospect of a Victory bond being drawn. Or, again, the expectation of life is only slightly uncertain. Even the weather is only moderately uncertain. The sense in which I am using the term is that in which the prospect of a European war is uncertain, or the price of copper and the rate of interest twenty years hence, or the obsolescence of a new invention, or the position of private wealth-owners in the social system in 1970. About these matters there is no scientific basis on which to form any calculable probability whatever. We simply do not know.

Keynes's central claim is that some of the time, we cannot assign probabilities to imaginable outcomes. "We simply do not know." Keynes immediately added, however, that "the necessity for action and for decision compels us as practical men to do our best to overlook this awkward fact and to behave exactly as we should if we had behind us a good Benthamite calculation of a series of prospective advantages and disadvantages, each multiplied by its appropriate probability, waiting to be summed."

How on earth, he wondered, do we manage to do that? Keynes listed three techniques:

(1) We assume that the present is a much more serviceable
guide to the future than a candid examination of past experience would show it to have been hitherto. In other words
we largely ignore the prospect of future changes about the
actual character of which we know nothing.

(2) We assume that the existing state of opinion as expressed
in prices and the character of *existing* output is based on a
*correct* summing up of future prospects, so that we can accept it as such unless and until something new and relevant
comes into the picture.

(3) Knowing that our own individual judgment is worthless,
we endeavor to fall back on the judgment of the rest of
the world, which is perhaps better informed. That is, we
endeavor to conform with the behavior of the majority or
the average. The psychology of a society of individuals each
of whom is endeavoring to copy the others leads to what we
may strictly term a *conventional* judgment.

Keynes did not mean to celebrate those techniques. He
thought that they were ridiculous. "All these pretty, polite
techniques, made for a well-panelled Board Room and a
nicely regulated market, are liable to collapse," because "we
know very little about the future."

Keynes's discussion describes a problem, and it is real.
But I have four concerns about his brief, exquisitely written
treatment. First, we often do know a lot about the future,
at least for the purposes of policy and law. Second, we can
learn more than we now know. Instead of making a stab in
the dark, we might want to wait and learn. Third, it is too

simple, often, to say that "we simply do not know." There are some relevant things that we do know. Fourth, we need to know how to handle situations in which it is true, or close to true, that "we simply do not know." It is not enough to disparage current techniques as pretty and polite. My main aim here is to put these concerns about Keynes's discussion in contact with an enthusiastic endorsement of his claim that, in important situations, we know far too little to make good Benthamite calculations.

There are approaches that are not exactly pretty, but that qualify as polite. They can save humanity a lot of distress.

# 1

## What We Don't Know

In the face of a pandemic threatening to produce numerous deaths, should aggressive preventive measures be undertaken, even if we cannot specify the benefits of those measures? Should cities, states, and nations be locked down? Exactly when and how? Should people be required to wear masks?

Imagine that some new technology, such as artificial intelligence, poses a catastrophic risk, but that experts cannot say whether the risk is very small, very large, or somewhere in between.[1] Should regulators ban that technology? Or suppose that genetically modified foods pose a risk of catastrophe—very small, but not zero.[2] Should officials forbid genetically modified foods? Should they require them to be labeled?

Suppose that scientists say that climate change will produce a range of possible outcomes by 2100, but that they cannot specify the likelihood of those outcomes. Should public officials assume the worst?[3] Should the social cost of carbon, designed to capture the damage from a ton of carbon emissions, reflect worst-case scenarios, and if so, exactly how?[4] Robert Pindyck describes the challenge this way:[5]

The design of climate change policy is complicated by the considerable uncertainties over the benefits and costs of abatement. Even if we knew what atmospheric GHG concentrations would be over the coming century under alternative abatement policies (including no policy), we do not know the temperature changes that would result, never mind the economic impact of any particular temperature change, and the welfare effect of that economic impact. Worse, we do not even know the probability distributions for future temperatures and impacts, making any kind of benefit–cost analysis based on expected values challenging to say the least.

Let us underline these thirteen words: "we do not even know the probability distributions for future temperature and impacts." If we do not even know that, how shall we proceed?

## Eight Conclusions

With a focus on public policy and regulation, my goal here is to help answer such questions. Among other things, I will be exploring possible uses of the *maximin principle*, which calls for choosing the approach that eliminates the worst of the worst-case scenarios. To see how the principle works, imagine that you face a risk that could produce one of three outcomes: (a) a small loss, (b) a significant loss, and (c) a catastrophic loss. The risk could come from genetic modification of food, nuclear power, a terrorist attack, a pandemic, an asteroid, or climate change. As I shall understand it here, the maximin principle says that you should take steps to avert the catastrophic loss. In life, as in public policy, that principle focuses attention on the very worst that might happen, and it argues in favor of eliminating it.

The maximin principle has been subject to formidable objections, especially within economics. An obvious concern is that eliminating the worst case might be extremely costly, and it might impose worst-case scenarios of its own. If you spend the next week trying to avert worst-case scenarios, you will create a lot of problems for yourself. I will be emphasizing and attempting to fortify the standard objections here. Nonetheless, one of my goals is to show that the maximin principle deserves a place in regulatory policy. I shall attempt to specify the circumstances in which it deserves that place. A central point is that sometimes regulators lack important information. Much of the discussion will be abstract, and based on stylized examples, but I shall ultimately make a number of concrete proposals, designed for real-world problems.

My starting point is simple: In extreme situations, public officials of diverse kinds must decide what kinds of restrictions to put in place against low-probability risks of catastrophe or risks that have terrible worst-case scenarios, but to which probabilities cannot (yet) be assigned. Some people, of course, favor quantitative cost-benefit analysis, whereas others favor some kind of Precautionary Principle. I am going to be embracing the former here, at least as a general rule,[6] but the claims that deserve emphasis involve the exceptions, which may call for precautionary thinking in general and for the maximin principle in particular.

This short book will cover a great deal of ground, and it will be useful to specify the basic conclusions at the outset. The first four are straightforward. The remaining four are not.

(1) To the extent feasible, policymakers should identify the likely costs and benefits of various possible outcomes.[7] They should ask about the harms associated with those outcomes and the probability that they will occur. They should aim to come up with probability distributions, accompanied by point estimates. When they cannot produce probability distributions, they should try to come up with reasonable ranges of both costs and benefits. They should do that partly to reduce the risk that political judgments will be based on intuitions, dogmas, or interest-group pressures. For example, people's intuitions are often a product of the availability heuristic, by which their judgments about risks depend on what events come readily to mind. Use of the availability heuristic can lead people to be unduly frightened of low-level risks and unduly complacent about potentially catastrophic risks (including the risks associated with horrific outcomes that are not on people's viewscreen).

(2) In deciding what to do, policymakers should focus on the *expected value* of various options: the potential outcomes multiplied by the probability that they will occur. In general, they should pick the option with the highest expected value. The qualification is that they might want to create a *margin of safety*, recognizing that it might itself impose serious burdens and costs. To avoid harm, a

degree of risk aversion may well make sense—but not if it is too costly and not if it imposes risks of its own. Insurance may be worth buying, but sometimes its price is too high.[8] (As we shall see, we might need a margin of safety against the risks created by margins of safety—a point that raises questions for those who like margins of safety.)

(3) In some cases, the worst cases are sufficiently bad, and sufficiently probable, that it will make sense to eliminate them, simply in terms of conventional cost-benefit analysis. That appears to have been the case for aggressive responses to the coronavirus pandemic in 2020.[9] That is, the benefits of those responses justified the costs. (It is natural to ask: How aggressive, exactly? How aggressive is too aggressive? Aggressive in what way? Those are the right questions, and the best answers pay close attention to both costs and benefits.)

(4) In some cases, the worst-case outcomes are highly *improbable*, but they are so bad that it may make sense to eliminate them under conventional cost-benefit analysis. Even though they are highly improbable, they might have an outsized role when regulators are deciding what to do. That is a reasonable view about costly efforts to reduce the risk of a financial crisis.[10] That is, such a crisis is highly unlikely (in any particular year), but its costs are so high that it is worthwhile to take (costly) steps to prevent one.[11] Again, this is standard cost-benefit analysis, based on expected values.

(5) In some circumstances, often described as Knightian uncertainty, observers (including regulators) cannot as-

sign probabilities to imaginable outcomes, and for that reason the maximin principle is appealing. I will argue that contrary to a vigorously defended view in economics, the problem of uncertainty is real and sometimes very important. For emphasis: Among economists, it is often claimed that Knightian uncertainty does not exist. That claim is wrong, and Knight was right (as was Keynes and as is Pindyck). In significant domains, we cannot assign probabilities to the possible outcomes.

(6) In some cases, the probability of extreme, very bad events is higher than normal;[12] it might make sense to eliminate those very bad outcomes, perhaps using conventional cost-benefit analysis, perhaps not. Some important problems involve "fat tails," for which the probability of a rare, bad event declines relatively slowly as that event moves far away from its central tendency. The fact that complex systems are involved can be important here; consider pandemics.

(7) In some cases, we do not know how fat the tail is or how bad the extreme, very bad event might be. Critical information is absent. Here as well, the maximin principle might have appeal.

(8) With respect to (5), (6), and (7), the problems arise when efforts to eliminate dangers would also impose very high costs or eliminate very large potential gains. If regulators spent a large percentage of gross domestic product on eliminating the risk of pandemics, they would probably do more harm than good. In addition, there might be extreme events of another sort, suggesting the possibil-

ity of wonders or miracles,[13] which might make human life immeasurably better and whose probability might be reduced by aggressive regulation. In deciding whether to impose such regulation on (for example) new technologies, it is important to keep wonder and miracles in mind.

## Ignorance and Maximin

This is a long and complicated list, so let us simplify it. In general, public officials should attempt to make human life better, which means that they should maximize social welfare (bracketing for the moment complex questions about what exactly that means).[14] To do that, they should calculate costs and benefits, with probability distributions as feasible and appropriate, and they should proceed if and only if the benefits justify the costs, perhaps incorporating a degree of risk aversion.[15] They should also focus on fair distribution—on who is being helped and who is being hurt—either because it is part of the assessment of social welfare, or because it is independently important. They should not focus solely or mostly on the worst cases; they should not give them more weight than other cases (bracketing for now risk aversion or loss aversion, to which I shall turn in due course). At the same time, calculation of costs and benefits may not be feasible, and an important question remains: Are there any problems that the maximin principle can handle better than welfare maximization?

The best answer is a firm "no," but it is too simple. One reason involves cases of Knightian uncertainty, where probabilities cannot be assigned. As we shall also see, the maximin principle is especially appealing when the costs of eliminating the worst-case scenario are not terribly high and when the worst-case scenario is genuinely grave. Consider, for example, the following cases:

1. *A nation faces a potential pandemic. It does not know the probability that the pandemic will occur. If it takes three steps, it can eliminate the danger. The three steps are not especially costly.*

2. *Over the next decade, experts believe that a nation is at risk of a serious terrorist attack. They do not know the probability that it will occur. But they believe that certain security measures at airports will substantially diminish the danger. Those measures are not especially costly.*

3. *Over the next decade, experts believe that a nation is at risk of a financial crisis. They do not know the probability that it will occur. They also believe that new capital and liquidity requirements, imposed on financial institutions, will make a financial crisis far less likely. Those requirements are burdensome, but their costs are manageable.*

In all of these cases, policymakers ought to give serious consideration to the maximin principle. As we shall see, the argument for use of that principle grows stronger as the badness of the worst-case scenario increases. It grows weaker as the costs of eliminating the worst-case scenario rise and as that scenario becomes decreasingly grave.[16]

There are no simple rules here. Judgments, not calculations, are required, and ideally, they will come from a well-functioning democratic process. But even when judgments are required, they can be bounded by applicable principles, which can prevent a lot of trouble.

# 2

# With and Without Numbers

Sometimes ordinary people do not have a lot of knowledge. Consider the case of COVID-19. What, exactly, are the benefits of wearing a mask? The risks of going on the subway? The same thing is true of policymakers. Consider the case of climate change, where it is worth quoting Pindyck at length:[1]

> One of the two more important uncertainties pertains to the extent of warming (and other aspects of climate change) that will occur given current and expected future GHG emissions. The second uncertainty pertains to the economic impact of any climate change that might occur, an impact that depends critically on the possibility of adaptation. Although various estimates are available, we simply don't know how much warmer the world will become by the end of the century under the Paris Agreement, or under any other agreement. Nor do we know how much worse off we will be if the global mean temperature increases by 2°C or even 5°C.
>
> In fact, we may never be able to resolve these uncertainties (at least over the [next] few decades). It may be that the extent of warming and its impact are not just unknown, but also unknowable. . . . When assessing climate sensitivity, we at least have scientific results to rely on, and can argue coherently about the probability distributions that are most

consistent with those results. When it comes to the predict-
ing the impact of climate change, however, we have much less
to go on, and the uncertainty is far greater. In fact, we know
very little about the impact that higher temperatures and ris-
ing sea levels would have on the economy, and on society
more generally. . . . So how likely is a catastrophic outcome,
and how catastrophic might it turn out to be? How high can
the atmospheric $CO_2$ concentration be before the climate
system reaches a "tipping point," and temperatures rise rapidly? We don't know.

Pindyck sounds a lot like Keynes here, though Keynes was
making a general point about problems that policymakers
(and the rest of us) sometimes face. If we don't know, what
should we do?

For many reasons, governments, private institutions, and
individuals might pay too little attention to catastrophic
risks. Many people suffer from "present bias"; they focus on
today and tomorrow, and not on the long term. They might
ignore a risk whose full force will be faced in decades or
more. We have also seen that people assess risks by using
the availability heuristic, asking whether relevant examples
come to mind. A catastrophic risk might well be one that
happens very infrequently, which means that people might
think that it need not be taken seriously; consider financial
crises or pandemics. People also tend to be unrealistically
optimistic, which might mean that they will give some risks
far less attention than they deserve. People also tend to think
that growth of various sorts is linear rather than exponential.

For some risks, including that of a pandemic, "exponential growth neglect" can lead people to discount the real danger, as happened in the early stages of the COVID-19 pandemic of 2020.[2] But my main topic here is how to think about appropriate responses, not behavioral science.

## Doctors

To see how to approach options in the face of serious gaps in information, let us turn to a very different kind of case. Imagine that you have a heart condition but that you would like to continue doing strenuous exercise. Perhaps you play tennis. You ask your doctor for advice, and she says that you probably should not play tennis, pointing to the risk of some kind of heart damage, which would in turn increase the risk of a stroke or a heart attack. Suppose that you ask her to assign probabilities to the range of possibilities, from "no adverse health effects at all" to "death." Suppose that she answers, "Okay, you've got me! The likelihood of no adverse health effects is very high—probably more than 99%. The likelihood of adverse health effects is in the vicinity of 1%, probably less. The likelihood of death, as a result of the strenuous exercise that you propose, is trivially small."

Under such circumstances, you may or may not continue playing tennis. An important question is how much you like doing it. You might want to weigh the psychological and other benefits of playing tennis (including how much fun it is to do it) against the very small chance of significantly increasing your health risks. The outcome of that weighing will depend on your preferences—on what you enjoy or care about. If you do not much enjoy tennis, you might decide, on precautionary grounds, to stop doing it. If tennis is something that much matters to you, you might continue. Things will get more complicated if your doctor adds, parenthetically, that if you continue to play tennis, there is some chance that you will get significant health benefits and thus *reduce* the risk of death. (The COVID-19 pandemic offers many examples of problems of this kind, as, for example, when people resume certain activities, increasing health risks.)

Now suppose, instead, that in response to your request that she assign probabilities to the various outcomes, she says, "I can't do that! No doctor can. For you, we just don't know enough about the likelihood of any of the outcomes, including the bad ones." What should you do? It would be reasonable to think: *I really need to get another doctor! Surely one of them has more information than that. Surely someone knows something about the probabilities.*

That would be a reasonable thought. But let us assume that the doctor is saying that this is a situation of Knightian uncertainty, in which, it will be recalled, probabilities cannot be assigned to various outcomes. Under such circumstances, some people would be drawn to the maximin principle: Adopt an approach that eliminates the worst-case scenario. With respect to pandemics, climate change, and regulation of new technologies, the same might be true. At least when some risk or technology has a terrible or catastrophic worst-case scenario, the best course might be to avoid it (depending on the costs and consequences of doing that).

Consider a real-world case encountered by a friend of mine. He has a mild heart condition. His doctor told him that his annual risk of a stroke is about 1.3%. If he goes on a medication, he can cut that risk to under 1%. (How much under? The science does not say.) But the medication itself creates a risk of serious complications—not nearly as serious as a stroke, but serious. What is the magnitude of that risk? The science suggests that it is under 1%. (How much under? The science does not say.) The doctor recommended that my friend go on the medication, using something like the maximin principle: A stroke is the worst-case scenario, and it should be avoided. My friend declined, on the theory that the trouble of taking a pill every day, combined with the risk of serious complications, exceeded the (small) benefit of reducing a stroke risk by just 4 in 1,000 (or perhaps a bit more). In my view, the doctor was reasonable in suggesting that my friend follow the maximin principle—but my friend was also reasonable in declining to do so.

## Assigning Probabilities

To understand the policy problem, or for that matter medical risks, we have to understand what it means to assign or to refuse to assign probabilities to future events. If a doctor refuses to do that, the simplest reason is that she lacks enough information. She might not have the data. She might think that no one does. (In the case of the medication to reduce the stroke risk, the doctor thought exactly that, in the sense that she believed that the science suggested that the medication would reduce the risk from 1.3% to 0.9% or well below, but without allowing assignment of probabilities.)

When someone refuses to assign probabilities, she might have a frequentist understanding of probability, in accordance with which she normally asks: In a large number of cases like this, how many times are there adverse health effects? This is the kind of question that someone might ask in assigning a probability to a fair coin coming up heads in 100 straight tosses, or a particular baby, born in Princeton, New Jersey, on August 29, turning out to be female. When a doctor or regulator refuses to assign probabilities, the reason might be that she is a frequentist, and she might not have the kinds of information that frequentists require.[3]

An alternative understanding of probability judgments is Bayesian, and it does not depend on knowledge of frequencies.[4] It can even be used for singular or unique cases.[5] Bayesian approaches might be used when someone says that the probability of a pandemic five years from now is under 2%, that the probability that the Democratic nominee for the US presidency will win is 50%, or that the probability of a particular set of outcomes in 2100, as a result of climate change, is over 90%. Bayesians start with a prior probability and then update on the basis of what they learn. Unlike frequentists, they are willing to assign probabilities to singular or nonrepeatable events. At the same time, a Bayesian doctor or regulator might agree that, in a particular case, any subjective probability that she assigns to an event is speculative in the extreme; she might acknowledge that she lacks sufficient information to have any confidence in it. For that reason, she might agree that the situation is one of Knightian uncertainty.

It is important to note that frequentists believe that for genuinely unique or nonrepeatable events, assignments of probability are essentially meaningless.[6] In their view, we have no basis for assigning a probability when we lack a frequency distribution. To say that a particular Democratic nominee has a 50% chance of being president, or that climate change is 90% likely to cause specified damage by 2100, is to speak nonsense, unless either statement can plausibly be justified in frequentist terms. For frequentists, the problem of Knightian uncertainty is therefore pervasive; it exists whenever we are dealing with a unique or nonrepeating problem, and we are doing that much of the time.[7]

In my view, frequentists are unconvincing on that count. It is not nonsensical to specify a probability that an event will occur even if we do not have a frequency distribution. But it is unnecessary to defend that conclusion for present purposes. Bayesians should also be willing to agree that, in some circumstances, Knightian uncertainty does indeed exist (a point to which I will return).

## Gaps in Knowledge

Consider in this regard a document from the White House, *Principles for Regulation and Oversight of Emerging Technologies*, issued in 2011 and still in effect.[8] (I was a coauthor of the document, and with apologies and a salute to my coauthors, I am going to raise doubts about it.) In general, the document embraces cost-benefit analysis, but in a puzzlingly qualified way:[9]

> *Benefits and costs: Federal regulation and oversight of emerging technologies should be based on an awareness of the potential benefits and the potential costs of such regulation and oversight, including recognition of the role of limited information and risk in decision making.*

What, exactly, is the role of limited information? What is the role of risk? With respect to regulation, the document explicitly calls out the problem of uncertainty:

> *The benefits of regulation should justify the costs (to the extent permitted by law and recognizing the relevance of uncertainty and the limits of quantification and monetary equivalents).*

The two italicized sentences are different. The first refers to limited information and risk. The second refers to uncertainty and the limits of quantification. But with respect to some problems, including those potentially raised by pandemics, climate change, and emerging technologies, we should understand the document, taken as a whole, to be emphasizing the epistemic limits of policymakers and regulators, and also to be drawing attention to the problem of Knightian uncertainty. These limits, and that problem, can be seen as qualifications to the general idea, pervasive in federal regulation, that regulators should proceed with a new regulation only if its benefits justify its costs.[10]

OMB Circular A-4, a kind of bible for federal regulatory analysis in the United States, explicitly recognizes both epistemic limits and Knightian uncertainty, and offers a plea for developing probability distributions to the extent feasible.[11] But what if it is not feasible to produce probability distributions, either because we lack frequencies or because Bayesian approaches cannot come up with them?

For a glimpse at the problem, consider a few numbers from annual cost-benefit reports of the Office of Information and Regulatory Affairs, the regulatory overseer in the Executive Office of the President.

(1) The projected annual benefits from an air pollution rule governing motor vehicles range from $3.9 billion to $12.9 billion.[12]

(2) The projected annual benefits of an air pollution rule governing particulate matter range from $3.6 billion to $9.1 billion.[13]

(3) The projected benefits of a regulation governing hazardous air pollutants range from $28.1 billion to $76.9 billion.[14]

(4) The projected benefits of a regulation governing cross-state air pollution range from $20.5 billion to $59.7 billion.[15]

It is worth pausing over three noteworthy features of those numbers. *First*, the government does not offer probability estimates to make sense of those ranges. It does not say that the probability at the low end is 1%, or 25%, or 50%. The default implication may be that the probability distribution is normal, so long as it is not specified, which might mean that the point forecast is the mean of the upper and lower bound. But is that really what is meant?

*Second*, the ranges are exceptionally wide. In all four cases, the difference between the floor and the ceiling is much higher than the floor—which is in the billions of dollars! (The technical term here is: Wow.)

*Third*, the wide ranges suggest that the worst-case scenario from government inaction, understood as a refusal to regulate, is massively worse than the best-case scenario. If regulators focus on the worst-case scenario, the relevant regulation is amply justified in all of these cases; there is nothing to discuss. The matter becomes more complicated if regulators focus on the best-case scenario or on the midpoint. But where should they focus?

All of these examples involve air pollution regulation, where projection of health benefits depends on significantly different models, leading to radically different estimates.[16] There appears to be a great deal of scientific uncertainty. But even outside of that context, relatively standard regulations, not involving new technologies, often project wide ranges in terms of benefits, costs, or both.[17] In terms of monetized costs, the worst case may be *double* the best case.[18] In terms of monetized benefits, the best case may be *triple* the worst case.[19] For a more general glimpse, consider this table, with particular reference to the wide benefits ranges:[20]

TABLE 1: Estimates of Annual Benefits and Costs of Non-Environmental-Related Health and Safety Rules: October 1, 2003–September 30, 2013

(billions of 2001 and 2010 dollars)

| Area of Safety and Health Regulation | Number of Rules | Estimated Benefits | | Estimated Costs | |
|---|---|---|---|---|---|
| | | 2001$ | 2010$ | 2001$ | 2010$ |
| Safety rules to govern international trade | 3 | $0.9 to $1.2 | $1.0 to $1.4 | $0.7 to $0.9 | $0.9 to $1.1 |
| Food safety | 5 | $0.2 to $9.0 | $0.3 to $10.9 | $0.2 to $0.7 | $0.3 to $0.9 |
| Patient safety | 7 | $12.8 to $21.9 | $12.8 to $21.9 | $0.9 to $1.1 | $1.1 to $1.4 |
| Consumer protection | 3 | $8.9 to $20.7 | $10.7 to $25.0 | $2.7 to $5.5 | $3.2 to $6.6 |
| Worker safety | 5 | $0.7 to $3.0 | $0.9 to $3.6 | $0.6 | $0.7 to $0.8 |
| Transportation safety | 24 | $13.4 to $22.7 | $15.4 to $26.4 | $5.0 to $9.5 | $6.0 to $11.4 |

Some of these gaps are very big, but for pandemics, climate change, and new technologies, the difference between the worst and the best cases is (much) bigger still.[21] It is also important to emphasize that new or emerging technologies may be or include "moonshots," understood as low-probability (or uncertain-probability) outcomes with extraordinarily high benefits; recall that we might call them miracles. Regulation might prevent those miracles,[22] or make them far less likely. In this domain, we may have "catastrophe-miracle" tradeoffs. It would not be at all good to prevent miracles from happening; they might make life immeasurably better (and longer). It is essential to attend to extreme downsides, but extreme upsides should not be neglected. In cases that involve new technologies, miracles might be in the offing, and we need to weigh them in the balance.

Because of its relevance to pandemics, climate change, and regulation of emerging technologies, I focus throughout on the difference between risk and uncertainty and urge that in the context of risk, adoption of the maximin principle is usually (not always) a fundamental mistake. Everything depends on the particular numbers, but in general, I aim to bury that rule, not to praise it.

At the same time, I suggest that it deserves serious attention under identifiable conditions. When regulators really are unable to assign probabilities to outcomes, and when some possible outcomes are catastrophic, the maximin principle can have considerable appeal. Climate change is at least a candidate for this conclusion,[23] and something similar might be said for some pandemics and other new or emerging risks, including some that are not even on the horizon.[24] But a great deal depends on what is lost by adopting the maximin principle. As we will see, catastrophic risks—of low or uncertain probability—might accompany both regulation and nonregulation.

# 3

# The Maximin Principle

Does it *generally* make sense to eliminate the worst-case scenario? Is that the right thing to do for genetically modified food? For nuclear power? For COVID-19? Put the question of uncertainty to one side and begin with numerical examples that involve risk instead. My topic is policy and regulation, of course, but to make conceptual progress on that problem, it will be useful to provide stylized cases involving monetary gambles, which have the advantage of stripping away possible complications. My hope is that the stylized cases can give us some clarity about how to approach real-world problems. At various points, I will try to show how these cases, however barebones, map onto such problems, involving air pollution, climate change, COVID-19, terrorism, and much more.

## Problems

PROBLEM 1.

Which would you prefer?

(a) A 99.9% chance of gaining $10,000, and a 0.1% chance of losing $60; or

(b) A 50% chance of gaining $50, and a 50% chance of losing $50.

Under the maximin principle, (b) is preferable, but under standard accounts of rationality, it would be much more sensible to select (a), which has a far higher expected value (outcome multiplied by probability). To choose (b), one would have to show an extraordinary degree of risk aversion. Now if losing $60 was far worse than losing $50—if it meant the difference between life and death—the argument for (b) would start to look less implausible. That (remote) possibility tells us something important, and we will return to it. But let's not quibble: (a) is much better.

Some policy problems have exactly this form. We might, for example, pursue an occupational safety policy that looks like (a), where it is overwhelmingly likely that we will save many lives, or instead one that looks like (b), where we have an even chance of gaining a little or losing a little. Sensible regulators choose (a).

PROBLEM 2.

Which would you prefer?

(a) A 70% chance of gaining $100, and a 30% chance of losing $30; or

(b) A 50% chance of gaining $10, and a 50% chance of losing $10.

Under maximin, (b) is again preferable, but under standard accounts of rationality, it would still be much more sensible to select (a), which has a much higher expected value. We could easily proliferate examples, in which the magnitude of risk aversion required to justify selection of (b) would be steadily reduced. For example:

PROBLEM 3.
Which would you prefer?
- (a) A 60% chance of gaining $600, and a 40% chance of losing $400; or
- (b) A 50% chance of gaining $100, and a 50% chance of losing $100.

Here again, (a) has higher expected value, but it is less obvious that a chooser should choose it, at least if this is the only gamble that she will be offered (a point to which I will return), and at least if the welfare loss of losing $400 is serious, even though the monetary figure is not so high.[1] If we added three zeros to the dollar figures in Problem 3, (b) might start to look better; the prospect of losing $400,000 might be very daunting.

Examples of this kind can also be mapped onto regulatory problems. For example, a decision to mandate widespread use of some new technology (say, electric cars) might take the form of Problem 2, where (a) is a mandate and (b) is no mandate. This could be so if we are not sure about the social costs and social benefits of such a mandate and can speak only in terms of probabilities. Similarly, a decision to allow widespread use of some new technology (say, artificial intelligence in cancer treatment) might take the form of Problem 3, where (a) is universal use and (b) is only partial adoption. This could be so if the reliability of the new technology is not clear.

In life or in public policy, is risk aversion irrational? If one is making a very large number of monetary bets, it certainly can be. If you had 100,000 questions like those immediately above, you should almost certainly choose (a). No gambler will do well if she keeps choosing (b).[2] But in some circumstances, the answer is less obvious. Suppose that a 70-year-old investor, Smith, is not in the best of health, and is deciding between two strategies for his pension. The first, called Caution, creates a 50% chance of no gain (aside from keeping up with inflation) and a 50% chance of an annual gain of 2%. The second, called Risky, creates a 25% chance of an annual loss of 5%, a 25% chance of no gain (aside from keeping up with inflation), a 25% chance of a 5% annual gain, and a 25% chance of a 10% annual gain.

In terms of expected value, Risky is much better. But without knowing about the effects of these outcomes on the chooser's welfare, it is hard to know which Smith should choose. There is the matter of worry: Would Risky cause fear and sleeplessness? Then there is the matter of economics: How much would a 5% loss matter to Smith? What would be the effect of a 10% gain? Perhaps a 5% loss would be devastating, given Smith's needs and wants, and perhaps a 10% gain would not much matter. Whether risk aversion is rational depends on the answer to these kinds of questions. The monetary figures are insufficient, because they do not tell us about the effects on Smith's welfare. The analysis is similar to those in the heart disease examples with which I began. Something similar might be true in the regulatory context; we need to know what the gains and the losses actually mean, in terms of welfare.

And what happens if the worst cases are catastrophically bad?

> PROBLEM 4.
>
> Which would you prefer?
>
> (a) A 99.9% chance of gaining $60, and a 0.1% chance of losing $200 million (resulting in a negative expected value); or
>
> (b) A 50% chance of gaining $10, and a 50% chance of losing $10.

Even if we know everything we need to know, (b) is better, certainly in terms of expected value. The example shows that a low-probability risk of catastrophe can drive the outcome of cost-benefit analysis, even if the probability is low indeed, and even if we put risk aversion to one side.

Calling attention to "fat tails," Martin Weitzman has emphasized the need to attend to catastrophic outcomes in the context of climate change.[3] The problem of fat tails is not captured in Problem 4; fat tails consist of a distinctive set of probability distributions, in which *there are very large departures from ordinary variations.*[4] In many circumstances, regulators are dealing with a normal distribution or a bell curve, in which probabilities get very low or start to vanish as we get further from the center. As an analogy, consider the height of human beings. Hardly anyone is going to be over eight feet tall; in human history, there have been only ten recorded cases. We can be pretty sure that no one is going to exceed nine feet.

But in some situations, policymakers (and the rest of us) are not dealing with normal distributions. Some highly unlikely events are far from the center, but when tails are fat, such events are much more likely than in normal distributions. A probability distribution is said to have fat tails if it declines to zero more slowly than exponentially.[5] As Nordhaus puts it, fat tails occur "when there are occasionally extremely large deviations from the normal range of variations in a variable such as stock price changes or earthquake size. If people are accustomed to a normal level of background variability, they may be very surprised, and sometimes badly hurt, by these tail events."[6]

Note that if we know the probability distribution, we should be able to do standard cost-benefit analysis. Suppose, for example, that we know that a massive change in stock market prices has a specified probability, or that the same is true of a catastrophically large earthquake or catastrophic damage from climate change. We can plug in the numbers. With a thin-tailed distribution, we can conclude that the very extreme outcomes are highly unlikely or even impossible, which means that the value of preventing them will be correspondingly low. With a fat-tailed distribution, the very extreme outcomes are not impossible and so cannot be dismissed, which means that the value of preventing them will be correspondingly higher. The extreme outcomes need real attention. We would pay more for preventing them, even without risk aversion; and if we are risk averse, we would pay more still. In terms of knowing what to do, the problem is compounded if we lack important information—if we know, for example, that extreme outcomes cannot be ruled out, but we do not know how probable they are.

Consider this:

PROBLEM 5.

Which would you prefer?

(a) A 95% chance of gaining $60, a 4% chance of losing $10, and a 1% chance of losing $900 million; or

(b) A 50% chance of gaining $10, and a 50% chance of losing $10.

Problem 5 (a) involves a (known) very fat tail, and (b) is much better in terms of expected value. Whether we are dealing with low-probability risks of catastrophe or fat tails, the magnitude of the potential harm can call for serious caution.[7] Nordhaus notes that something like this captures reality, for in some situations, "the probability of the 'way-out' events occurring" turns out to be "much greater than predicted by the normal distribution."[8] The point may apply to significant problems, including those involving pandemics and risky technologies. (In such cases, the fact that we are dealing with complex systems, and unpredictability about how they will work, may be exceptionally important.)

Consider Weitzman's suggestion, focusing on climate change:[9]

Deep structural uncertainty about the unknown unknowns of what might go very wrong is coupled with essentially unlimited downside liability on possible planetary damages. This is a recipe for producing what are called "fat tails" in the extremes of critical probability distributions. There is a race being run in the extreme tail between how rapidly probabilities are declining and how rapidly damages are increasing. Who wins this race, and by how much, depends on how fat (with probability mass) the extreme tails are. It is difficult to judge how fat the tail of catastrophic climate change might be because it represents events that are very far outside the realm of ordinary experience.

In this passage, Weitzman combines an emphasis on "the unknown unknowns," or uncertainty, with a reference to "the extremes of critical probability distributions."[10]

Problems 4 and 5 do not involve a fundamental lack of information or uncertainty. They point only to extreme outcomes, which can be enough to dominate the comparison of expected values. These, then, are cases in which the maximin principle might be justified on the ground that it does *not* conflict with what would emerge from an analysis of expected value; because of the sheer magnitude of the harm in the worst-case scenario, it has outsized importance in the judgment about what to do. (To be sure, risk-seeking choosers might take their chances with (a)). As I have noted, this might be the right analysis of certain pandemics, especially when we emphasize the possibility (probability?) of exponential growth in infections and deaths.

Note, however, that variations on Problem 4 are imaginable and illuminating. If we add a lack of knowledge to the mix (deep structural uncertainty about unknown unknowns) and also add risk aversion, the argument for eliminating the danger might turn out to be very strong—a point to which I will return.

Or consider this:

> PROBLEM 6.
> Which would you prefer?
> (a) A 99.9% chance of gaining $60, and a 0.1% chance of losing $200 million; or
> (b) A 49.9% chance of gaining $10, a 50% chance of losing $10, and a 0.1% chance of losing $100 million.

Problem 6 shows that low-probability, high-magnitude risks might accompany more than one option. Both action and inaction might pose low-probability, high-magnitude risks. On one view (with admittedly contested assumptions), climate change is an example. Immediate, very costly steps might be necessary to avert catastrophic risks, but they might themselves impose catastrophic risks, if (for example) they might threaten to create some massive economic downturn and geopolitical instability. (We could easily alter Problems 5 and 6 so as to include uncertainty.) With respect to new or emerging technologies, of course, there may be potentially massive upsides as well as potentially catastrophic downsides. Artificial intelligence and machine learning are possible examples.[11] In that regard, consider this:

PROBLEM 7.

Which would you prefer?

(a) A 51% chance of gaining $60, and a 49% chance of losing $1; or

(b) A 49.9% chance of gaining $10, a 50% chance of losing $10, and a 0.1% chance of gaining $100 million.

This is a problem of the "moonshot" or "miracle," understood to involve an option with a low-probability chance of producing extraordinary returns.[12] If the potential returns are high enough, the expected value might justify choosing that option. Here again, Problem 7 could be altered so as to include uncertainty.

We could also imagine cases in which an option has a *negative* expected value, but in which the moonshot might nonetheless be thought to be an appealing gamble. Suppose, for example, that for $1,000, you can buy a very small chance of a truly extraordinary payoff whose expected value is less than $1,000. Is it so clear that you should not buy that chance? One question is the welfare loss produced by losing $1,000. And if (b) in Problem 7 is combined with (a) in Problem 4, we will face "catastrophe-miracle" tradeoffs, here in circumstances of risk. (With uncertainty, the analytical challenge is even harder, though if catastrophes are bad enough—say, extinction—they may justifiably loom larger than miracles.)

What about the option of inaction? Every one of the foregoing problems could be understood to *include* inaction as one of two options, producing one of the relevant payoffs, or could be designed so as explicitly to include that option. A simple example, where (b) is understood to mean inaction:

PROBLEM 8.

Which would you prefer?

(a) A 50% chance of gaining $1.5 million, and a 50% chance of losing $1 million; or
(b) A 50% chance of gaining or losing nothing, and a 50% chance of losing $500,000.

In terms of expected value, (a) is better. But in a one-shot gamble, the right choice might not be so clear. One more time: For individuals, a gain of $1.5 million may produce less welfare than would be lost by a loss of $500,000. There is a difference between expected monetary value and expected utility (or welfare). Once we transform money into welfare, (b) might start to look more attractive, even if we put loss aversion (taken up shortly) to one side.

Consider an attempt to broaden the viewscreen:

PROBLEM 9.

Which would you prefer?

(a) A 50% chance of losing $100 million, and a 50% chance of losing $200 million; or
(b) An 80% chance of losing $50 million, and a 20% chance of losing $90 million.

Option (b) is obviously better, though both are bad. (I am understanding the numbers as net losses, compared to the status quo.) We need not speak of the maximin principle in order to reach that conclusion. In 2020, the coronavirus pandemic could easily have been analyzed in terms of Problem 9, with (some) aggressive responses producing (b), and much less aggressive responses producing (a).[13] Problem 9 is instructive because it shows that when aggressive regulation and nonregulation (understood to include weak regulation) *both* impose significant and even catastrophic net losses, an understanding of standard cost-benefit analysis can call for aggressive regulation.

Now consider a different case, explicitly involving Knightian uncertainty:

PROBLEM 10.

Which would you prefer?

(a) A 100% chance of losing $1; or

(b) A 100% chance of gaining $100,000, alongside a chance of dying.

In this case, the chance is unspecified. You do not know whether it is 99%, or 50%, or 0.1%. You might choose option (a), on the ground that you are not losing all that much compared to the status quo (though giving up a gain of $100,000 is not exactly trivial), and the loss associated with (b) is potentially catastrophic. Of course, you might also want to invest something in learning what that chance is, but maybe you don't have time to do that, and maybe learning is not possible in the short term.

Or consider this:

PROBLEM 11.

Which would you prefer?

(a) A 100% chance of losing $1; or

(b) A 100% chance of gaining $100,000, alongside a chance of getting sick.

In this case, you do not know either the probability of getting sick or the gravity of the illness, if you get it. (Technically, you are facing a situation of *ignorance*, because both probabilities and outcomes are unknown.) Here again, you might well be drawn to (a), because you seek to avoid a possibility of dying, and losing $1 really isn't that bad. That would seem to be a perfectly reasonable choice. Now consider a different kind of problem.

PROBLEM 12.

Which would you prefer?

(a) A 100% chance of getting $1,000; or

(b) A chance of getting $1,000, and a chance of getting more than $1,000, without information about how probable it is that you will get $1,000, or how probable it is that you will get more than $1,000.

It should be clear that (b) is better than (a). If you choose (b), you will at worst do as well as you would by choosing (a), and possibly better. This is a radically simplified case of *breakeven analysis*, which is an exceedingly valuable tool for choosers who lack information. With breakeven analysis, people start by asking: What is the level of benefits that

I would have to obtain to make it worthwhile to incur the cost? Then they ask: What is the lowest amount of benefits that I will obtain in the worst case, or the highest in the best case? If they can answer that question, they might well know how to proceed. They might know that the lower bound, with respect to benefits, is higher than the cost, or that the upper bound is lower than the cost. If so, the decision is obvious.

There are many regulatory analogues. Suppose that an effort to reduce smoking would save 500 lives, at a minimum, and that it would cost $800 million. Because a statistical life is valued at $10 million, that is an excellent expenditure. Or suppose that an effort to reduce air pollution would save 50 lives, at a maximum, and that it would cost $2 billion. That would seem to be an unjustified expenditure. In the face of gaps with respect to benefits or costs, or both, breakeven analysis often tells people how to proceed—and if the gaps in information are such that it cannot even do that, at least its use enables us to see what makes some cases very hard, and also to specify exactly what information people need to obtain to make some cases easier.

One final problem (and it is a bit more exotic than the previous 12):

PROBLEM 13.
An evil supernatural being has come to earth and told you, credibly: "Thanks to me, you have a problem: You might die tomorrow morning. I won't tell you the probability; it might be 0.01%, it might be 99.99%, it might be

50%. I will remove that problem for a price. How much would you pay me to remove it?"

This is a very hard problem to handle. Unfortunately, nothing in decision theory seems to help much. If you face a number of serious mortality risks and can avoid them for a reasonable price, you might want to attend to them first. If you have higher priorities than your own life, you will certainly focus on them (at least if you can do so before you die). Suffice it to say that there is no strictly logical answer to the question posed by the evil supernatural being.

# 4

# The Precautionary Principle

For certain regulatory problems, many people accept the Precautionary Principle.[1] The idea takes multiple forms, some far more cautious and targeted than others,[2] but it is often understood to embody a general commitment to risk aversion. The central idea is that regulators should take aggressive action to avoid certain risks, even if they do not know that those risks will come to fruition.

Suppose, for example, that there is some probability that genetic modification of food will produce serious environmental harm.[3] For those who embrace the Precautionary Principle, it is important to take precautions against potentially serious hazards, simply because it is better to be safe than sorry. Thus the 1992 Rio Declaration states, "Where there are threats of serious or irreversible damage, lack of full scientific certainty shall not be used as a reason for postponing cost-effective measures to prevent environmental degradation."[4] The Wingspread Declaration goes somewhat further: "When an activity raises threats of harm to human health or the environment, precautionary measures should be taken even if some cause and effect relationships are not fully established scientifically. In this context the proponent of an activity, rather than the public, should bear the burden of proof."[5]

Whatever the preferred formulation, the Precautionary Principle can be seen as an effort to build in a kind of margin of safety, perhaps because of "a clear normative presumption in favour of particular values or qualities—for instance concerning [the] environment or human health. This is instead of (for example) economic, sectoral, or partisan institutional interests."[6] In certain forms, the principle might be taken to reflect the maximin principle: Rule out the worst of the worst-case scenarios. But insofar as we are speaking about risk aversion in general, the Precautionary Principle runs into a serious objection: risks may be on all sides of social situations. Regulators are often dealing with *risk-risk tradeoffs* or even *health-health tradeoffs*.[7] When this is so, it is not helpful to speak of "a clear normative presumption in favour of . . . human health," at least when human health is at risk whatever choice regulators make.[8]

Suppose, for example, that steps are taken to regulate or ban genetically modified food on precautionary grounds.[9] Some people believe that any such steps might well result in numerous deaths and a small probability of many more.[10] The reason is that genetic modification holds out the promise of producing food that is both cheaper and healthier—potentially resulting, for example, in "golden rice," which might have large benefits in developing countries.[11] The point is not that genetic modification will definitely have those benefits, or that the benefits of genetic modification outweigh the risks, or that precautions are a bad idea. The point is only that if the Precautionary Principle is taken in certain ways, it is offended by regulation as well as by nonregulation. To be sure, the maximin principle might prove helpful here on a certain set of empirical assumptions—an issue to which I will return.

Or consider regulation of autonomous vehicles.[12] There is no question that such vehicles pose risks to public safety. Some of them crash. At the same time, a failure to allow autonomous vehicles, or even to promote them, or perhaps even to *mandate* them, might well be seen to offend the Precautionary Principle because the result would be, with some probability, to cost lives.[13] Use of autonomous vehicles might well increase safety, perhaps dramatically. We are dealing with safety-safety tradeoffs. The example shows again that if it is understood in a certain way, the Precautionary Principle seems to forbid the very steps that it requires. To make progress, it would seem necessary, not to speak of precautions or to invoke maximin, but to identify the possible outcomes and to specify the probability that they will occur. That will rapidly move us in the direction of cost-benefit analysis. But what if important information is absent?

To see how hard that question might bite, imagine that technical analysts inform political officials that if they proceed with a regulation, the monetized benefits will have a range of $300 million to $1.5 billion, and that the monetized costs will have a range of $200 million to $1.6 billion. (The example is not so artificial; in the context of genetically modified food, for example, the Department of Agriculture projected first-year costs of between $600 million and $3.6 billion.[14]) Suppose that the analysts add that they cannot assign probabilities to various points within the range. We seem to have not only a risk-risk tradeoff, in the sense that risks lie on both sides of the problem, but also an uncertainty-uncertainty tradeoff, in the sense that analysts identify outcomes without probabilities on both sides.[15] Should we say that the agency should not proceed, because $1.6 billion is higher than $1.5 billion? That is hardly clear.

## Danger

Now turn to a mundane illustration of the kinds of decisions in which the maximin principle might seem attractive: A reporter, living in Los Angeles, has been told that she can take one of two assignments. First, she can go to a nation, say Syria, in which conditions are dangerous (perhaps because there is a military conflict). Second, she can go to Paris to cover anti-American sentiment in France. The Syria assignment has, in her view, two polar outcomes: (a) she might have the most interesting and rewarding experience of her professional life or (b) she might be killed. The Paris assignment has two polar outcomes of its own: (a) she might have an interesting experience, one that is also a great deal of fun or (b) she might be lonely and homesick.

It might seem tempting for the reporter to choose Paris, on the ground that the worst-case scenario for that choice is so much better than the worst-case scenario for Syria. To know if this is so, she should probably think a bit about probabilities. She might not have numbers, but she might know enough to know, roughly, that the chance of being killed in Syria is quite small, but higher than in Paris, and that she would worry about that risk while in Syria. These points might incline her, reasonably enough, to choose Paris. And if this is correct, the conclusion might bear on regulatory policy, where one or another approach has a conspicuously worse worst-case scenario.[16] To be sure, regulators would want to be more disciplined about both outcomes and probabilities.

But we have seen enough to know that maximin is not always a sensible decision rule. Suppose that the reporter now has the choice of staying in Los Angeles or going to Paris; suppose too that on personal and professional grounds, Paris is far better. It would make little sense for her to invoke maximin in order to stay in Los Angeles on the ground that the plane to Paris might crash. A plane crash is of course extremely unlikely, but it cannot be entirely ruled out. Using an example of this kind, John Harsanyi contends that the maximin principle should be rejected on the ground that it produces irrationality, even madness: "If you took the maximin principle seriously you could not ever cross the street (after all, you might be hit by a car); you could never drive over a bridge (after all, it might collapse); you could never get married (after all, it might end in a disaster), etc. If anybody really acted in this way he would soon end up in a mental institution."[17]

Harsanyi's argument might also be invoked to contest the use of maximin in the choice between Syria and Paris. Perhaps the reporter should attempt to specify the likelihood of being killed in Syria, rather than simply identifying the worst-case scenario and resting content with intuitive assessments. Perhaps maximin is a way of neglecting probability, and hence a form of irrationality. In some circumstances, people do display probability neglect, in a way that ensures attention to the worst-case scenario.[18] But if probabilities can actually be assessed, and if that scenario is extremely unlikely to come to fruition, probability neglect is hard to defend even for people who are exceptionally risk averse. Suppose that the risk of death in Syria turns out to be 1 in 1,000,000, and that the choice of Syria would be much better, personally and professionally, than the choice of Paris.

Importantly, it is necessary to know something about the reporter's values and tastes to understand how to resolve this problem, but it is certainly plausible to think that the reporter should choose Syria rather than make the decision by obsessively fixating on the worst that might happen. The Council of Environmental Quality once required but no longer requires worst-case analysis; it refuses to do so on the ground that extremely speculative and improbable outcomes do not deserve attention.[19] So far, then, Harsanyi's criticism of maximin seems on firm ground.

But return in this light to the Precautionary Principle and notice that something important is missing from Harsanyi's argument and even from the reporter's analysis of the choice between Los Angeles and Paris. Risks, and equally bad worst-case scenarios, are on all sides of the hypothesized situations. If the reporter stayed in Los Angeles, she might be killed in one way or another, and hence the use of maximin does not by itself justify the decision to stay in the United States. And contrary to Harsanyi's argument, the maximin principle does not really mean that people should not cross streets, drive over bridges, and choose to marry. The reason is that failing to do those three things has worst-case scenarios of its own (including death and disaster). To implement the maximin principle, or an injunction to take precautions, it is necessary to identify all relevant risks (including both outcomes and probabilities), not a subset.

Nonetheless, the more general objection to the maximin principle holds under circumstances of risk. We have seen that if probabilities can be assigned to the various outcomes, it usually does not make sense to follow maximin and to reject an option that contains a terrible worst-case scenario, if that scenario is exceedingly improbable and if the likelihood of an excellent outcome is very high. As noted, many people are risk averse, or averse to particular risks, and on welfare grounds, some kinds of risk aversion, or aversion to particular risks, might be a good idea for individuals and societies. But when probabilities can be assigned, the maximin principle, imposed rigorously, seems to require infinite risk aversion.[20]

Compare this choice: (1) Have a one-week family vacation in Florida, where it would be a great deal of fun, but where there is a 0.0001% chance of being killed by a Burmese python or (2) stay home in Hartford, Connecticut, where it would be relatively boring. Option (1) contains (let us stipulate) the worst-case scenario, but does it really make sense to reject it for that reason? It follows that the reporter would do well to reject maximin, and go to Paris, even if the worst-case scenario for Paris is worse than that for Los Angeles *if* the realistically likely outcomes are so much better in Paris.

These points are not meant to suggest that in order to be rational, the reporter must calculate expected values, multiplying imaginable outcomes by probability and deciding accordingly. Life is short; people are busy and occasionally risk averse; anxiety and worry are themselves harms, and may cause harms; important information might be missing or unavailable; it is far from irrational to create a margin of safety to protect against disaster. But if the likelihood of a bad outcome is exceptionally small, and if much is to be gained by deciding in accordance with expected values, maximin is foolish. It does not make sense, as a general rule, to identify the worst-case scenario and to attempt to eliminate it. But the problem of uncertainty raises distinctive questions.

## OMB Circular A-4

For regulatory impact analysis in the US government, the key document is OMB Circular A-4, finalized in 2003.[21] That document offers a detailed discussion of how to proceed in the absence of complete information. It recognizes that "the level of scientific uncertainty may be so large that you can only present discrete alternative scenarios without assessing the relative likelihood of each scenario quantitatively. For instance, in assessing the potential outcomes of an environmental effect, there may be a limited number of scientific studies with strongly divergent results." It adds that "whenever possible, you should use appropriate statistical techniques to determine a probability distribution of the relevant outcomes. For rules that exceed the $1 billion annual threshold, a formal quantitative analysis of uncertainty is required."[22]

But that analysis might leave gaps, simply because insufficient information is available to produce specific numbers. In such cases, Circular A-4 offers guidance about how to proceed, calling for a "formal probabilistic analysis of the relevant uncertainties, possibly using simulation models and/or expert judgment." In such assessments, "expert solicitation is a useful way to fill key gaps in your ability to assess uncertainty. In general, experts can be used to quantify the probability distributions of key parameters and relationships. These solicitations, combined with other sources of data, can be combined in Monte Carlo simulations to derive a probability distribution of benefits and costs." Optimistically, Circular A-4 concludes: "You should make a special effort to portray the probabilistic results—in graphs and/or tables—clearly and meaningfully."[23]

It is safe to say that the ambition of this discussion has not been fulfilled. In the context of air pollution rules, which sometimes cost at least $1 billion, a formal probabilistic analysis is not usually offered. Instead, agencies tend to report ranges.[24] There might be some pragmatic judgments in the background here. Agencies might be thinking that the analysis suggested by Circular A-4 is quite demanding, and if the benefits of a rule exceed the costs on any reasonable assumptions, the costs of undertaking the analysis might exceed the benefits. But without investigating particular problems in detail, we cannot know whether that is true. And in some cases, involving new risks and emerging technologies, the approach suggested by Circular A-4 might well be the right way to go.

Suppose, for example, that the technical analysis converges on these conclusions: *The cost of a regulation is $1 billion. The benefits range from $800 million to $1.3 billion.* The first step would be to see if the benefits range could be turned into some kind of point estimate. The second would be to see if probabilities could be assigned to various points along the range, perhaps with the use of the approaches outlined in OMB Circular A-4. Under the circular, the agency should be pressed to do exactly that.

## What Is Going on Here?

In a provocative and spirited book, Kay and King are very hard on the idea of maximizing expected value, urging that we often do not know enough to do anything like that.[25] Instead of generating numbers, they urge that regulators, officials, and others should ask, "What is going on here?" They also ask for close attention to "narratives." The problem is that the "What is going on here?" question cannot easily yield sensible answers. How can regulators possibly know how to handle (say) clean air, food safety, pandemics, nanotechnology, and genetic modification of food, if that is their question? The analysis is best disciplined through at least a rough sense of both probabilities and outcomes, which is often obtainable; lacking those, maximin is a candidate solution.

Revealingly, Kay and King defend the "What is going on here?" question in part by reference to President Barack Obama's decision to authorize the raid to kill Osama Bin Laden without knowing that Bin Laden was actually present in the relevant location. In my view (and I was in the White House at the time, though not involved in any way with the decision), this is not a helpful example; it counts strongly against the central argument offered by Kay and King. Obama's decision was Bayesian, and it involved a careful assessment of costs and benefits (and hence expected value). Roughly: The benefits of killing Bin Laden would be very high; the costs of failing would be high but manageable; the likelihood that he was present fell within an ascertainable range (in the vicinity of 50%); and importantly, the likelihood that he would be found, in the short-term future, seemed relatively low. My experience is that public officials approach many nonrepeatable events in this way, by thinking about outcomes and probabilities, not by asking, "What is going on here?"

Kay and King rightly draw attention to the importance of resilience and robustness as ways of handling uncertain risks. Consider the risks associated with climate change and pandemics. But how resilient, and how robust? Resilience and robustness can be very costly indeed. We would not want to spend infinite costs, today, to create resilience against a pandemic in a decade. Under conditions of risk, calculation of expected value can be more than helpful; as we shall see, maximin has its place. "Narrative," by contrast, is of limited use.

William Nordhaus offers wise words here:[26]

In many cases, the data speak softly or not at all about the likelihood of extreme events. This means that reasonable people may have quite different views about the likelihood of extreme events, such as the catastrophic outcomes of climate change, and that there are no data to adjudicate such disputes. This humbling thought applies more broadly, however, as there are indeed deep uncertainties about virtually every issue that humanity faces, and the only way these uncertainties can be resolved is through continued careful consideration and analysis of all data and theories.

In the midst of those "quite different views" held by reasonable people, what is necessary is some kind of decision rule, pending acquisition of more knowledge. It is tempting to rule out worst-case scenarios, but as in life, so in regulatory policy: yielding to temptation might have high costs, including worst cases of its own.

## Loss Aversion

People tend to be loss averse, which means that they view a loss from the status quo as more undesirable than they view an equivalent gain as desirable.[27] When we anticipate a loss of what we now have, we can become genuinely unhappy or afraid, in a way that greatly exceeds our feelings of pleasure when we anticipate some (equivalent) addition to what we now have. So far, perhaps, so good. The problem comes when individual and social decisions downplay potential gains from the status quo and fixate on potential losses, in such a way as to produce overall increases in risks and overall decreases in well-being. The problem is heightened by the possibility that loss aversion is an "affective forecasting error"—that is, people might think (at the time of decision) that losses will have a much greater effect on their well-being than they actually do (in experience).[28]

In the context of risk regulation, there is a clear implication: People will be closely attuned to the losses produced by any newly introduced risk, or by any aggravation of existing risks, but far less concerned with the benefits that are foregone as a result of regulation. The point very much bears on decisions of the Food and Drug Administration, where the risks of allowing unsafe or ineffective drugs on the market may be quite visible, while the risks of not allowing potentially safe and effective drugs on the market may be hidden. (This asymmetry was put under a great deal of pressure in connection with the COVID-19 pandemic; it was clear to all that delaying a vaccine could have very high costs, including numerous deaths.) The point bears on the introduction of new technologies more broadly, where regulators might be highly attuned to the risks of allowing them (and imposing losses) and less attuned to the risks of forbidding them (and failing to obtain gains).

More generally, loss aversion often helps to explain what makes the Precautionary Principle operational. The benefits eliminated or foregone as a result of regulation may register little or not at all, whereas the threats posed by the activity or substance in question may be highly visible. In fact, this is a form of status quo bias.[29] The status quo marks the baseline against which gains and losses are measured, and a loss from the status quo seems much worse than a gain from the status quo seems good.

If loss aversion is at work, we would predict that the Precautionary Principle would place a spotlight on the losses introduced by specified risks and downplay the benefits foregone as a result of controls on the sources of those risks. Recall the emphasis, in the United States, on the risks of insufficient testing of medicines as compared with the risks of delaying the availability of those medicines. If the "opportunity benefits" are offscreen, the Precautionary Principle will appear to give guidance notwithstanding the objections I have made. At the same time, the neglected opportunity benefits sometimes present a serious problem with the use of the Precautionary Principle.

Loss aversion is closely associated with another cognitive finding: people are far more willing to tolerate familiar risks than unfamiliar ones, even if they are statistically equivalent.[30] For example, the risks associated with driving often do not produce a great deal of concern, even though in the United States alone, more than 30,000 people die from motor vehicle accidents each year. The relevant risks are seen as part of life. By contrast, many people are quite concerned about risks that appear newer, such as the risks associated with genetically modified foods, recently introduced chemicals, and terrorism. Part of the reason for the difference may be a belief that, with new risks, we think that we are in the domain of uncertainty rather than risk, and perhaps we think that it makes sense to be cautious when we are unable to measure probabilities. But the individual and social propensity to focus on new risks outruns that potentially sensible thought.

It makes the Precautionary Principle operational by emphasizing a subset of the hazards actually involved.

At first glance, it is tempting to think that if regulators fall prey to loss aversion, they will blunder. Consider a situation in which autonomous ("self-driving") vehicles will produce 25 deaths that would not have occurred, but prevent 500 deaths that would have occurred. Unless those numbers conceal other factors, it seems clear that autonomous vehicles should be allowed. That is indeed the right result, but if people are loss averse, they might give more weight to a loss resulting from a new technology than they give to a loss resulting from the status quo. Because loss aversion bears on public reactions, and because the public might be outraged or frightened by deaths that would not otherwise have occurred, regulators might have to work carefully to prevent beneficial new technologies from being discredited.

To test these questions, I conducted a survey on Amazon's Mechanical Turk, asking about 400 demographically diverse people to assume that in a city in their state, officials were deciding whether to go forward with a pilot project allowing automated vehicles on the road. Then I presented respondents with this scenario:

*Imagine that the experts project that if automated vehicles are allowed, they would be responsible for 15 accidents that would not have otherwise occurred, during the next six months—but that automated vehicles would also prevent 50 accidents that would otherwise have occurred, in those next six months.*

The question was whether the project should go forward. Fully 84% said "yes." When I changed the numbers to 20/30 (for another group), a strong majority (74%) again said "yes." A strong majority appears not to be loss averse, at least in the sense that they think that the right question is simple: What approach would produce fewer overall accidents?

In general, the majority is correct on that point. But for some dangers, there is a countervailing consideration. If things go very badly, we might have a catastrophe. If things go very well, we might have a miracle. Reasonable regulators might want to prevent a possible catastrophe, even if the price is to prevent a possible miracle. The downside risk of (say) extinction might reasonably be seen to deserve more attention than the upside potential of (say) immortality.

## The Mythical Benevolence of Nature

Sometimes the Precautionary Principle operates by incorporating the belief that nature is essentially benign and that human intervention is likely to carry risks—as in the suggestion that the Precautionary Principle calls for stringent regulation of man-made pesticides and chemicals. This can be seen as a distinctive form of loss aversion. The idea is that human intervention might create losses from the status quo and that those losses should carry great weight, whereas the gains should be regarded with some suspicion or at least be taken as less weighty. Often, loss aversion and a belief in nature's benevolence march hand in hand: The status quo forms the baseline or reference state against which to assess deviations. To many people, processes that interfere with nature are a troubling "degradation."

A belief in the benevolence of nature does seem to play a role in the operation of the Precautionary Principle, especially among those who see nature as harmonious or in balance. In fact, many of those who endorse the principle seem to be especially concerned about new technologies. Many people believe that natural chemicals are safer than man-made chemicals. (Most toxicologists disagree.) On this view, the principle calls for caution when people are intervening into the natural world. Here, of course, we can find considerable sense: Nature often consists of systems, and interventions into systems can cause a number of problems. New technologies can produce unintended bad effects, if only because they interfere with systems. But there is a large problem with this understanding of the Precautionary Principle: What is natural may not be safe at all.

Consider, for example, the idea that there is a "balance of nature." According to one account, this idea is "not true."[31] A "scientific revolution" has shown that nature "is characterized by change, not constancy,"[32] and that "natural ecological systems are dynamic," with desirable changes being "those induced through human action."[33] In any case, nature is often a realm of destruction, illness, killing, and death. Hence the claim cannot be that human activity is necessarily or systematically more destructive than what nature does.[34] Nor is it clear that natural products are comparatively safe. Some of the most serious risks are a product of nature. Tobacco smoking kills over 400,000 Americans each year; the Precautionary Principle might be (but has not been) directed against it. Nothing is more natural than exposure to sunlight, but such exposure is associated with skin cancer and other harms, producing serious health problems that have not been the occasion for invoking the Precautionary Principle.

To say this is not to resolve specific issues, which depend on complex questions of value and fact. My only suggestion is that the false belief in the benevolence of nature helps to explain why the Precautionary Principle is thought, quite incorrectly, to provide a great deal of analytical help. It is much better to try to get clear on the relevant numbers. But what if we can't?

# 5

# Uncertainty

Now let us turn to what are, in a sense, the largest issues. Recall Keynes's claim about some situations: "We simply do not know." Recall, too, Pindyck's words about key issues raised by climate change: "We do not know." In March 2020, it was possible that if experts were asked about the likely number of deaths from COVID-19, many would have said, "We do not know." If experts are asked about the likely number of deaths from climate change by 2100, that might not be a bad answer, and the same is true if people are asked about the number of lives lost between the years 2050 and 2090 as a result of pandemics.

It is also true that in some contexts, risk-related problems involve hazards of ascertainable probability. It might be possible to say that the risk of death from a certain activity is 1 in 100,000, or at least that it ranges from (say) 1 in 20,000 to 1 in 100,000, with an exposed population of (say) 10 million. Or it might be possible to say that the risk of catastrophic harm from some activity is under 5% but above 1%. Recall the case of my friend's doctor, who said, on the basis of the best available evidence, that a medicine could reduce an annual stroke risk from 1.3% to "below 1%."

But as we have seen, it is possible to imagine instances in which analysts cannot specify even a range of probability, easily or at all,[1] perhaps because they are frequentists who cannot find relevant frequencies, perhaps because they are Bayesians who lack necessary information. Once again: Regulators, and ordinary people, are sometimes acting in situations of Knightian uncertainty (where outcomes can be identified but no probabilities can be assigned) rather than risk (where outcomes can be identified and probabilities assigned to various outcomes).

Indeed, they are sometimes acting under conditions of ignorance, in which they are unable to specify either the probability of bad outcomes or their nature—where regulators do not even know the magnitude of the harms that they are facing.[2] One reason might be that they are dealing with a unique or nonrepeatable event. Another reason might be that they are dealing with a problem involving interacting components of a system, in which regulators cannot know how the components are likely to interact with each other.[3]

## Strategies of Avoidance

Of course, learning is possible. Over time, some problems that involve ignorance might turn into problems of uncertainty, and problems of uncertainty might turn into problems of risk—a point that may well counsel in favor of delay while new information is received. You would not want to spend $5 trillion to eliminate a danger if you could spend $1 billion on research, learning its magnitude in a reasonable time. If the cost of eliminating an uncertain danger is very high, it could make much more sense to find out something about the probability that it will come to fruition.

OMB Circular A-4 emphasizes this point: "For example, when the uncertainty is due to a lack of data, you might consider deferring the decision, as an explicit regulatory alternative, pending further study to obtain sufficient data."[4] But as the circular notes, "Delaying a decision will also have costs, as will further efforts at data gathering and analysis."[5] Delay of regulation may mean serious harm (including large numbers of deaths; consider the coronavirus pandemic of 2020). In principle, agencies would calculate the costs and benefits of delay. But because of the very problem that counsels in favor of delay (lack of information), that calculation may not be possible.

It is also true that agencies might use *breakeven analysis*, discussed above, to make progress in the face of uncertainty (at least if it is bounded).[6] Suppose, for example, that the costs of regulation are $100 million, that the benefits range from $800 million to $2 billion, and that technical analysts state that, at the present time, they cannot assign probabilities to the lower or upper bound, or to points along the range. Even so, it is clear that the regulation should go forward. Or suppose that the monetized costs of some new technology (say, a variation on fracking) are $500 million, but that the monetized benefits range from $600 million to $10 billion. A regulatory ban would not be a good idea. We could easily imagine variations on these numbers. Breakeven analysis can enable regulators to identify reasonable paths forward even in the midst of uncertainty.

The Principle of Insufficient Reason holds that when people lack information about probabilities (say, 1% to 40%), they should act as if each probability is equally likely.[7] There is some evidence that people follow that principle, at least in surveys.[8] But why is it rational to do that? By hypothesis, there is no reason to believe that each probability is equally likely. Making that assumption is no better than making some other, very different assumption. The Principle of Insufficient Reason is essentially arbitrary.[9]

## Into the Thicket

When strategies of avoidance are unappealing or unsuccessful, regulators might be drawn to the maximin principle: *Choose the policy with the best worst-case outcome.*[10] In the context of regulation of pandemics or new technologies, for example, perhaps elaborate precautions can be justified by reference to the maximin principle, asking officials to identify the worst case among the various options and to select that option whose worst case is least bad. Perhaps the maximin principle would lead to a Catastrophic Harm Precautionary Principle, by, for example, urging elaborate and expensive steps to combat especially serious risks. It follows that if aggressive measures are justified to reduce the risks associated with pandemics or emerging technologies, one reason is that those risks are potentially catastrophic and existing science does not enable us to assign probabilities to the worst-case scenarios. The same analysis might be applied to many problems, including the risks associated with geneti-cally modified food,[11] nuclear energy,[12] and terrorism.

To understand these claims, we need to back up a bit. I have suggested that maximin has sometimes been recom-mended under circumstances of uncertainty rather than risk.[13] In an influential discussion, John Rawls, focusing on justice, offers a justification for a rule that "directs our at-tention to the worst that can happen."[14] As he puts it, "this unusual rule" is plausible in light of "three chief features of situations."[15] The first is that we cannot assign probabili-ties to outcomes, or at least we are extremely uncertain of them (hence Knightian uncertainty). The second is that the chooser "has a conception of the good such that he cares very little, if anything, for what he might gain above the minimum stipend that he can, in fact, be sure of by following the maxi-min principle."[16] For that reason, it "is not worthwhile for him to take a chance for the sake of further advantage." The third is that "the rejected alternatives have outcomes that one can hardly accept." In other words, they involve "grave risks." Under the stated conditions, there is not much to be gained from running a catastrophic risk, which means that choos-ers should not much value those gains, and it is worthwhile giving them up to protect against a downside outcome that choosers deplore.

Rawls emphasizes that the three "features work most effec-tively in combination," which means that the "paradigm situ-ation for following the maximin principle is when all three features are realized to the highest degree."[17] That means that the rule does not "generally apply, nor of course is it self-evident."[18] It is "a maxim, a rule of thumb, that comes into its own in special circumstances," and "its application depends upon the qualitative structure of the possible gains and losses in its relation to one's conception of the good, all this against a background in which it is reasonable to discount conjectural estimates of likelihoods."[19]

Rawls's own argument is that for purposes of justice, the original position, as he understands it, is "defined so that it is a situation in which the maximin principle applies"[20]—which helps to justify his principles of justice. It is worthwhile noting that the same argument can help to identify situations in which the maximax principle applies, understanding that principle to counsel adoption of the option or approach that has the best best-case scenario. Assume, first, that people are acting under conditions of uncertainty, or close to it. Assume, second, that the chooser "has a conception of the good such that he cares greatly for what he might gain by following the maximax rule." Assume, finally, that grave or even significant risks are not involved, which is to say that if things go sour, and the chooser does not end up with the best possible outcome, he is nonetheless well enough off, given his conception of the good. In those circumstances, we should elect the option with the best best-case scenario, not the one with the worst worse-case scenario.

Putting maximax to one side, we can think of the cases on which Rawls is focusing as involving a horrible gamble: an option with which one can incur catastrophic losses of unknown probability but obtain no (real) gains.[21] Who wants that? In such cases, applying maximin seems quite rational. Recall Problem 10 from chapter 3:

> PROBLEM 10.
> Which would you prefer?
> (a) A 100% chance of losing $1; or
> (b) A 100% chance of gaining $100,000, alongside a chance of dying.

Rational people might choose (a), and that can be seen as a simplified version of Rawls's central claim.

## Precautions Again

These points bear on regulatory policy, where Rawls's defense of maximin has inspired a defense and reconstruction of the Precautionary Principle in an important essay by Stephen Gardiner.[22] To make the underlying intuition clear, Gardiner begins with the problem of choosing between two options, A and B:[23]

> If you choose A, then there are two possible outcomes: either (A1) you will receive $100, or (A2) you will be shot. If you choose B, there are also two possible outcomes: either (B1) you will receive $50, or (B2) you will receive a slap on the wrist. According to a maximin strategy, one should choose B. This is because: (A2) (getting shot) is the worst outcome on option A and (B2) (getting a slap on the wrist) is the worst option on plan B; and (A2) is worse than (B2).

It should be immediately apparent that if we can assign probabilities to outcomes, A might turn out to be the better choice. Suppose that if you choose A, there is a 99.99999% chance of (A1), and that if you choose B, there is a 99.99999% chance of (B2). If so, A might seem better. But let us stipulate that assignment of probabilities is not possible. In Gardiner's view, this conclusion helps support what he calls the Rawlsian Core Precautionary Principle in the regulatory setting: When Rawls's three conditions are met, precautions, understood as efforts to avoid the worst-case scenario, should be adopted. As he puts it: "If one really were faced with the genuine possibility of disaster, cared little for the potential gains to be made by avoiding disaster and had no reliable information about how likely the disaster was to occur, then, other things being equal, choosing to run the risk might well seem like a foolhardy and thereby extreme option."[24]

Gardiner adds, importantly, that to justify the maximin principle, the threat posed by the worst-case scenario must satisfy some minimal threshold of plausibility. In his view, "the range of outcomes considered are in some appropriate sense 'realistic,' so that, for example, only credible threats are considered."[25] If they can be dismissed as unrealistic, then maximin should not be followed. Gardiner believes that the problem of climate change (and also that of genetically modified organisms) can be usefully analyzed in these terms and that it presents a good case for the application of the maximin principle. As he puts it:[26]

The RCPP [Rawlsian Core Precautionary Principle] appears to work well with those global environmental issues often said to constitute paradigm cases for the Precautionary Principle, such as climate change and genetically-modified crops. For reasonable cases can be made that the Rawlsian conditions are satisfied in these instances. For example, standard thinking about climate change provides strong reasons for thinking that it satisfies the Rawlsian criteria. First, the "absence of reliable probabilities" condition is satisfied because the inherent complexity of the climate system produces uncertainty about the size, distribution and timing of the costs of climate change. Second, the "unacceptable outcomes" condition is met because it is reasonable to believe that the costs of climate change are likely to be high, and may possibly be catastrophic. Third, the "care little for gains" condition is met because the costs of stabilizing emissions, though large in an absolute sense, are said to be manageable within the global economic system, especially in relation to the potential costs of climate change.

We should underline here Gardiner's sensible suggestion that to justify maximin, the threats that are potentially catastrophic must satisfy some minimal threshold of plausibility.[27] Gardiner believes that the problem of climate change can be usefully analyzed in these terms and that it presents a good case for the application of maximin.[28] To be sure, there is a small conceptual puzzle here. If an outcome can be dismissed as unrealistic, then we are able to assign some probabilities, at least. Gardiner's argument must be that, in some cases, we might know that the likelihood that a bad outcome would occur really is trivial.

In a similar vein, Jon Elster, speaking of nuclear power, contends that maximin is the appropriate choice when it is possible to identify the worst-case scenario and when the alternatives have the same best consequences.[29] Recall the possibility of fat tails, containing extreme, very bad outcomes, where maximin might also be appealing. Without endorsing maximin, Pindyck suggests:[30]

> As a guide to policy, the conclusion that we should be willing to sacrifice close to 100 percent of GDP to reduce GHG emissions is not very useful, or even credible. . . . A more useful interpretation . . . is that with fat tails, traditional benefit–cost analysis based on expected values . . . can be very misleading, and in particular will underestimate the gains from abatement. It also implies that when evaluating or designing a climate policy, we need to pay much more attention to the likelihood and possible consequences of extreme outcomes.

A related argument, ventured by Nassim Nicholas Taleb et al. in an illuminating discussion and specification of the Precautionary Principle, is that genetically modified crops pose a "ruin" problem, involving a low probability of catastrophically high costs.[31] Taleb et al. contend that for such problems, it is best to take strong precautions—in this case, placing "severe limits" on genetically modified food. If the basic analysis is correct, the question is whether genetically modified crops really do create ruin problems. Perhaps they do, but it is also possible to read the most recent science to suggest that they do not; if the probability of catastrophic harm is vanishingly low and essentially zero, rather than merely very low, we can fairly ask whether Taleb's argument applies. If the risk of catastrophic harm can be dismissed, then maximin should not be followed.

But the larger point is that, in narrow but identifiable circumstances, the argument for the maximin principle seems plausible. Taken seriously, this conclusion would have real consequences for regulatory policy, potentially in the context of pandemics and climate change, and also in the context of new risks or emerging technologies. Recall the problems discussed in chapter 3; we have seen that in some of them, maximin has real appeal. I will give more examples, and specify the easy cases and the hard ones, in the conclusion.

# 6

# Objections

I now turn to five objections to the argument on behalf of using the maximin principle.

## The Argument Is Trivial

An evident problem with the argument for maximin is that it risks triviality.[1] If individuals and societies can eliminate an uncertain danger of catastrophe for essentially no cost, then of course they should eliminate that risk! If people are asked to pay $1 to avoid a potentially catastrophic risk to which probabilities cannot be assigned, they had better pay $1. And if two options, A and B, have the same best-case scenario, and if A has a far better worst-case scenario, people should of course choose A.

According to this objection, there is nothing wrong with the Rawls/Gardiner argument on behalf of maximin, but the real world rarely presents problems of this simple form. Where policy and law are disputed, the elimination of uncertain dangers of catastrophe imposes both costs and risks. In the context of climate change, for example, it is implausible to say that regulatory choosers can or should care "very little, if anything," for what might be lost by following maximin. If nations followed anything like the maximin principle for climate change, they would spend a great deal to reduce greenhouse gas emissions.[2] That might well be a good idea (and I think that it would be), but the result would almost certainly be higher prices for gasoline and energy, potentially producing increases in unemployment and poverty.

Something similar can be said about genetic modification of food, because elimination of the worst-case scenario, through aggressive regulation, might well eliminate a source of nutrition that might confer substantial benefits and that could have exceptionally valuable effects on numerous people who live under circumstances of extreme deprivation.[3] If we seek to eliminate the worst-case scenarios for all pandemic risks, people will simply be required to stay at home, today, tomorrow, and the day after. On imaginable assumptions, that might be the right approach. But the fact that a very bad worst-case scenario is associated with the pandemic (worse, let us stipulate, than the worst case associated with the stay-at-home mandate) cannot easily be taken to justify that mandate, unless we work to learn more about probabilities.

The real question, then, is whether regulators should embrace maximin in real-world cases in which doing so is costly or even extremely costly. Perhaps they should. In the Rawls/ Gardiner framework, it is stipulated that people will lose little or nothing by following the maximin principle. That is one reason that their argument in favor of the principle is so appealing; it also threatens to make their argument trivial. But even if the costs of following the maximin principle are significant, and even if regulators really do care about incurring those costs, the question is whether it makes sense to follow the maximin principle when citizens face uncertain dangers of catastrophe. In the environmental context, some people have so claimed.[4] They might be right; I will turn to their view in the conclusion. For the moment, their claim takes us directly to the next objection to maximin.

## Infinite Risk Aversion

Rawls's arguments in favor of adopting maximin, for purposes of distributive justice, were subject to withering critiques from economists—critiques that many economists accept to this day.[5] The central challenge was that the maximin principle would be chosen only if choosers showed *infinite risk aversion*. In the words of one of Rawls's most influential critics, infinite risk aversion "is unlikely. Even though the stakes are great, people may well wish to trade a reduction in the assured floor against the provision of larger gains. But if risk aversion is less than infinite, the outcome will not be maximin."[6]

In chapter 2, we saw the problem. To be concrete: Suppose that you have a choice between two options. Option A has a 99.9999% likelihood of yielding great wealth and welfare and a 0.0001% likelihood of a terrible outcome. Option B has a 60% chance of a very bad outcome and a 40% chance of a just-short-of-terrible outcome. Would it really make sense to choose Option B, on the ground that Option A has the worse worst-case? To adapt this objection to the regulatory context: It is plausible to assume a bounded degree of risk aversion with respect to catastrophic harms to support some modest forms of a Catastrophic Harm Precautionary Principle. Under that approach, we might take extra precautions to avoid catastrophe, if doing so is not terribly costly. But even under circumstances of uncertainty—the argument goes—maximin is senseless unless societies are to show infinite risk aversion.

This is a standard challenge, but it is wrong, because maximin does not assume infinite risk aversion.[7] By stipulation, *we are dealing with situations in which probabilities cannot plausibly be assigned to various outcomes.* Perhaps that is rare in the regulatory context. But in principle, the objection that maximin assumes infinite risk aversion depends on a denial that uncertainty exists; it assumes that subjective choices will be made and that they will reveal subjective probabilities. It is true that subjective choices will be made. But such choices do not establish that objective uncertainty does not exist. To see why, it is necessary to engage that question directly.

## Uncertainty Does Not Exist

Many economists have denied the existence of uncertainty.[8] Milton Friedman, for example, writes of the risk-uncertainty distinction that "I have not referred to this distinction because I do not believe it is valid. I follow L. J. Savage in his view of *personal probability*, which denies any valid distinction along these lines. We may treat people as if they assigned numerical probabilities to every conceivable event."[9] Friedman and other skeptics are correct to insist that people's choices suggest that they assign probabilities to events. On a widespread view, an understanding of people's choices can be taken as evidence of subjective probabilities. People's decisions about whether to fly or instead to drive, whether to go to a store or a movie during a pandemic, whether to walk in certain neighborhoods at night, and whether to take risky jobs can be understood as implicitly assigning probabilities to events. Indeed, regulators themselves make decisions, including decisions about climate change, from which subjective probabilities can be calculated.

But none of this makes for anything like a good objection to Knight, who was concerned with objective probabilities rather than subjective choices.[10] Animals, no less than human beings, make choices from which subjective probabilities can be assigned. I have two dogs (Labrador retrievers), and they make plenty of choices every day, some of them based on fear of harm (and others based on hope for food). But the existence of subjective probabilities—from dogs, horses, and elephants—does not mean that animals never face (objective) uncertainty.

Suppose that the question is the likelihood that at least 100 million human beings will be alive in 10,000 years. For most people, equipped with the knowledge that they have, no probability can sensibly be assigned. Perhaps uncertainty is not unbounded; the likelihood can reasonably be described as above 0% and below 100% (I think). But beyond that point, there is little to say. Or suppose that I present you with an urn, containing 250 balls, and ask you to pick one; if you pick a blue ball, you will receive $1,000, but if you pick a green ball, you will have to pay me $1,000. Suppose that I refuse to disclose the proportion of blue and green balls in the urn—or suppose that the proportion has been determined by a computer, which has been programmed by someone whom neither you nor I know. You can make a choice, but what does that tell us about actual probabilities? Regulators may be in a similar position at the early stage of a pandemic or when dealing with a new technology. These examples suggest that it is wrong to deny the possible existence of uncertainty, signaled by the absence of objective probabilities.

For Savage and other skeptics about uncertainty, there is an additional problem. When necessary, human beings do assign subjective probabilities to future events. So what? The assignment can be a function of how the situation is described, and formally identical descriptions can produce radically different judgments. There is reason to believe, for example, that people will not give the same answer to the question "What is the likelihood that 80% of people will suffer an adverse effect from a certain risk?" and to the question "What is the likelihood that 20% of people will not suffer an adverse effect from a certain risk?"[11] The merely semantic reframing may well affect probability judgments.[12]

In any case, probability judgments can be highly unreliable because they are frequently based on heuristics and biases that lead to severe and systematic errors.[13] Recall that subjective probability estimates can be rooted in the availability heuristic, leading people to exaggerate risks for which examples readily come to mind ("availability bias") and also to underestimate risks for which examples are cognitively unavailable ("unavailability bias").[14] Why should regulators believe that subjective estimates, subject as they are to framing, heuristics, and biases, have any standing in the face of the objective difficulty or impossibility of making probability judgments? (Note that unavailability bias can lead people to neglect the risk of catastrophes.)

Even if individuals and governments assign subjective probabilities, do their assignments bear on what ought to be done? As Elster puts it, speaking of scientists and bureaucrats: "There are too many well-known mechanisms that distort our judgment, from wishful thinking to rigid cognitive structures, for us to attach much weight to the numerical magnitudes that can be elicited by the standard method of asking subjects to choose between hypothetical options."[15] Even if this account is too pessimistic (as I think it is), there are some problems for which merely subjective probabilities cannot plausibly be taken to show that we are operating in circumstances of risk rather than uncertainty. In any case, recall the benefits ranges reported in chapter 2 above, in which officials declined to offer probability estimates, evidently on the ground that no adequate evidence could support them.

Recall that in 1937, Keynes, sometimes taken to be a critic of the idea of uncertainty, clearly saw the distinction between objective probabilities and actual behavior: "The sense in which I am using the term ['uncertain' knowledge] is that in which the prospect of a European war is uncertain. . . . About these matters there is no scientific basis on which to form any calculable probability whatever. We simply do not know."[16] Recall once more that this is so even if, as Keynes immediately added, we act "exactly as we should if we had behind us a good Benthamite calculation of a series of prospective advantages and disadvantages, each multiplied by its appropriate probability, waiting to be summed."[17] Even if subjective expected utilities can be assigned on the basis of behavior, regulators (like everyone else) may well be operating in circumstances of genuine uncertainty.

## Not Usual

Notwithstanding these points, regulatory problems do not typically involve uncertainty. Using frequentist strategies, regulators are often able to assign probabilities to outcomes, and Bayesian approaches can also be helpful. When they are not, perhaps regulators can instead assign probabilities to probabilities. In many cases, regulators might be able to specify a range of probabilities, saying, for example, that the probability of catastrophic outcomes from a pandemic or climate change is above 2% but below 30%.[18] Recall the doctor from chapter 2, who said that a medication would reduce the annual probability of a stroke from 1.3% to below 1%, without saying how much below 1% and without assigning probabilities to the various points below 1%.

Whatever we think of any particular example, perhaps we can agree that pure uncertainty is not usual.[19] Perhaps we can agree that, at worst, some regulatory problems involve problems of "bounded uncertainty," in which we cannot assign probabilities within specified bands. It is possible to think, for example, that the risk of a catastrophic outcome is above 1% but below 10% without being able to assign probabilities within that band. The pervasiveness of uncertainty depends on what is actually known. If uncertainty is rare, then Rawls's argument, or variations on it, do not apply outside of unusual cases. Fair enough. But even if this is so, unusual cases may turn out to be important, and perhaps the most important of all.

## Distributional Considerations

The final objection is not directed against maximin on its own terms. It urges that when thinking about catastrophe, or anything close to it, we need to focus on an issue to which I have not devoted much attention: who is being helped and who is being hurt. If there is a pandemic, who gets sick, and who dies? Does climate change disproportionately affect poor people in poor countries? These are critical questions. Or suppose that some technology promises miracles but also has horrific downsides. Who would benefit from the miracles, and who would be hurt by the downsides?

Some catastrophes, and some worst-case scenarios, pose special threats to people who are at the very bottom of the economic ladder. At least in some nations, the COVID-19 pandemic is an example, because poor people, and people of color, have been especially vulnerable. Something similar can be seen with environmental risks. Regulators should work long and hard to combat unfairness of this kind. But when we think about appropriate responses, one challenge is that precautionary and remedial measures may also come down especially hard on people who are at the bottom of the economic ladder. Closing the schools is not exactly an engine of equal opportunity. And if costly regulation, driven by the maximin principle, is imposed on sources of risk (such as fossil fuels and motor vehicles), it might well impose disproportionate hardship on the poor. The costs of regulation operate like a tax, and it can be a regressive one, with especially serious adverse effects on people who do not have much money. In my view, for example, a carbon tax is an excellent idea, but taken by itself, it harms the poor more than the wealthy.

It is correct and important to say that distributional issues matter. If a regulation has monetary costs in excess of monetary benefits, it might still be justified, if those who bear the costs are well-off and if those who enjoy the benefits are not.[20] This point holds whether or not we are dealing with catastrophic risks and whether or not we have significant gaps in information. But it does not argue in favor of or against the use of the maximin approach. It does suggest that when we know something about who is helped and who is hurt by precautions, or by the refusal to insist on precautions, we should take that knowledge into account in deciding what to do. Fairness matters.

# 7

## Irreversibility

A number of years ago, a close friend of mine lost her mother. When she told me the news, she added, "This is the first time, in my entire life, that the world has gone around the sun without my mother on it." Her remark was searing because the loss was irreversible. When you lose someone you love, the loss is forever. Of course, it is also true that if you have certain religious convictions, you might think, or even be sure, that you will see the person again. (Even if you don't have religious convictions, you might also think that, in some sense.) Even so, a death of a loved one produces mourning, and a kind of incredulity, simply because of its finality.

The COVID-19 pandemic produced global mourning, and global incredulity, because there was so much finality to the many losses for which it was responsible. And indeed, many problems have an element of irreversibility. If a species is lost, it is probably lost forever; the same might well be true of pristine areas. Genetically modified organisms might lead to irreversible ecological harm; transgenic crops can impose irreversible losses by increasing pest resistance.[1] In recent decades, the problem of climate change has raised the most serious concerns about irreversibility. Some greenhouse gases stay in the atmosphere for centuries, and for that reason climate change threatens to be irreversible, at least for all practical purposes.

Concerned about the problem of irreversibility, sensible nations might want to adopt a distinctive principle for handling certain kinds of risk: the Irreversible Harm Precautionary Principle. There is an obvious connection between irreversibility and the problem of catastrophe, though, as we shall soon see, a focus on the former offers a distinctive perspective and a fresh set of concerns.

Indeed, a concern with irreversibility seems to underlie prominent accounts of the Precautionary Principle, which point explicitly to that problem. For example, the United Nations Framework Convention on Climate Change proclaims: "Where there are threats of serious or irreversible damage, lack of full scientific certainty should not be used as a reason for postponing [regulatory] measures, taking into account that policies and measures to deal with climate change should be cost-effective so as to ensure global benefits at the lowest possible cost."[2] Recall that the 1992 Rio Declaration states, "Where there are threats of serious or irreversible damage, lack of full scientific certainty shall not be used as a reason for postponing cost-effective measures to prevent environmental degradation."[3]

In American environmental law, related ideas are at work. San Francisco has adopted its own Precautionary Principle, with an emphasis on irreversibility: "Where threats of serious or irreversible damage to people or nature exist, lack of full scientific certainty about cause and effect shall not be viewed as sufficient reason for the City to postpone cost effective measures to prevent the degradation of the environment or protect the health of its citizens."[4] At the federal level, the National Environmental Policy Act requires agencies to discuss "any irreversible and irretrievable commitments of resources which would be involved in [a] proposed action should it be implemented."[5] Courts have been careful to insist that environmental impact statements should be prepared at a time that permits consideration of environmental effects before irretrievable commitments have been made.[6] A number of other federal statutes, especially in the environmental context, specifically refer to irreversible losses and make their prevention a high priority.[7] Within the federal courts, a special Precautionary Principle has sometimes underlain the analysis of preliminary injunctions in cases involving a risk of irreparable environmental harm.[8]

As a first approximation, the Irreversible Harm Precautionary Principle offers a simple if vague claim: *Special steps should be taken to avoid irreversible harms, through precautions that go well beyond those that would be taken if irreversibility were not a problem.* The general attitude here is "act, then learn," as opposed to the tempting alternative of "wait and learn." At some points during the last decades, some people have argued that for climate change, further research should be our first line of defense. In the 1990s and 2000s, they argued that nations should refuse to commit substantial resources to reducing greenhouse gas emissions until evidence of serious harm became clearer. To be sure, this view seems to have fewer adherents every year. But some people continue to believe that our initial steps should be relatively cautious, increasing in aggressiveness as knowledge accumulates (and the costs of emissions reductions fall). In this domain, however, there is a large problem with any approach of "wait and learn." If precautionary steps are not taken immediately, the results may be irreversible, or at best difficult and expensive to reverse. For climate change, it might be best to take precautions now as a way of preserving flexibility for future generations.

My goal in this chapter is to explore the idea of irreversibility in the regulatory context, with special reference to environmental protection. In one sense, the notion is unhelpful, for any losses are irreversible, simply because time is linear. If Jones plays tennis this afternoon, rather than working, the relevant time is lost forever. If a project to drill oil in Alaska is delayed for five years, there is an irreversible loss as well: The oil that might have been made available will not be made available when it otherwise would have been. When environmentalists emphasize the importance of irreversibility, I suggest that they have two separate ideas in mind. The first is connected with the idea of option value and in particular with the view that when information is missing, it is worthwhile to spend resources to maintain future flexibility as knowledge increases. The second involves losses of goods that are incommensurable in that sense that they are qualitatively distinctive.

I shall focus throughout on the problem of climate change, because it has such evident importance and because it provides a good area for exploring the underlying puzzles. But as we shall see, the exploration of those puzzles bears on a wide range of questions about appropriate precautions, not only in the environmental arena, but in other legal domains and in daily life as well.

## Existence Value, Option Value

Let us begin with the monetary valuation of an environmental good, such as a pristine area. Some people will be willing to pay to use the area; they might visit it on a regular basis, and they might be very upset by its loss. But others will be willing to pay to preserve it, even if they will not use it. In fact, many citizens would be happy to give some money to save a pristine area, perhaps especially if animals can be found there. Hence "existence value" is sometimes included in the valuation of environmental goods,[9] and indeed federal courts have insisted that agencies pay attention to that value in assessing damages to natural resources.[10] Taken as a group, citizens of many nations would be willing to pay a great deal to preserve an endangered species or to maintain the existence of a remote island and its ecosystem. In fact, valuation of the damage from climate change must pay attention to the loss of species and animals, if only because human beings care about them.

But some people are also willing to pay for the *option* to use or to benefit from an environmental amenity in the future, even if they are unsure whether they will ever exercise that option.[11] Suppose that a pristine area might be developed in a way that ensures its permanent loss. Many people would be willing to pay a significant amount to preserve their option to visit that area. Under federal law, option value must also be considered in the assessment of natural resource damages.[12] Many regulations pay attention to option value in the environmental context.[13] For numerous goods, people are willing to pay and to do a great deal in order to ensure that their options are preserved.

Here, then, is a simple sense in which irreversible harm causes a loss that should be considered and that must be included in measures of value. Some skeptics contend that it "is hard to imagine a price for an irreversible loss,"[14] but people certainly do identify prices for such losses, or at least for the risk of such losses.[15] Whether or not we turn that value into some sort of monetary equivalent, it ought to matter.

The idea of option value is closely related to the use of the notion of "options" in the domain that I shall be emphasizing here. The simple claim is that when regulators are dealing with an irreversible loss, and when they are uncertain about the timing, magnitude, and likelihood of that loss, they should be willing to pay a sum—the option value—to maintain flexibility for the future. The option might not be exercised if it turns out that the loss is not a serious one. But if the option is purchased, regulators will be in a position to forestall that loss if it turns out to be large. The concern about irreversibility, and hence the Irreversible Harm Precautionary Principle, is based on the idea that regulators should be willing to buy an option to maintain their own flexibility. (I am using terms that suggest monetary payments, but the basic point holds even if we are skeptical about the use of monetary equivalents; "purchases" can take the form of precautionary steps that do not directly involve money.)

In the domain of finance, options take multiple forms.[16] An investor might be willing to purchase land that is known to have deposits of gold. Even if the cost of extraction is too high to justify mining, ownership of the land creates an option to mine if the cost falls.[17] A standard "call option" is a right to purchase an asset prior to a specific date at a specified price.[18] (People might pay for the right to buy a share of stock in their favorite company at $50 six months from now.) In another variation, people might seek the right to abandon a project at a fixed price, perhaps on the occurrence of a specified worst-case scenario. (People might agree to perform some service for someone, but obtain the right not to perform in the event of bad weather, bad health, or some other contingency.) Alternatively, people might obtain the right to scale back a project, to expand it, or to extend its life. Options that recognize multiple sources of uncertainty, of the sort that can be found for many environmental problems, are termed "rainbow options."[19]

Option theory has countless applications outside of the domain of investments. People would be willing to do and possibly even to spend a great deal to preserve their option to have another child—even if they are not at all sure that they really want to have another child. Or consider narrow judicial rulings, of the sort celebrated by judicial minimalists,[20] who want courts to make decisions that are focused on particular details and that leave many questions undecided. Narrow rulings can be understood as a way of "buying" an

option, or at least of "paying" a certain amount by imposing decision-making burdens on others, in return for future
flexibility. Judges who leave things undecided, and who focus
their rulings on the facts of particular cases, are in a sense
forcing themselves, and society as a whole, to purchase an
option to pay for flexibility in the resolution of subsequent
problems. Whether that option is worthwhile depends on
its price and the benefits that it provides. Or consider the
case of marriage and suppose that, because of law or social
norms, it is difficult to divorce, so that a decision to marry
cannot readily be reversed. If so, prospective spouses might
be willing to do a great deal to maintain their flexibility before marrying—far more than they would be willing to do if
divorce were much easier.

It should be readily apparent how an understanding of option value might explain the emphasis in the National Environmental Policy Act (NEPA) and other environmental
statutes on irreversible losses. The central point of NEPA is
to ensure that government officials give serious consideration
to environmental factors before they take action that might
threaten the environment.[21] If the government is building a
road through a pristine area, or drilling in Alaska, or licens-
ing a nuclear power plant, it must produce an "environmental impact statement" discussing the environmental effects.
The production of these statements can be burdensome and
costly. But when potentially irreversible losses are involved,
and when officials cannot specify the magnitude or likelihood of such losses, the public, and those involved in making
the ultimate decision, ought to know about them.

## Options, Imperfect Knowledge, and Precautions

It should now be clear that the idea of option value might help support the Irreversible Harm Precautionary Principle. The seminal essay was written by Kenneth Arrow and Anthony Fisher, who demonstrate that the ideas of uncertainty and irreversibility have considerable importance to the theory of environmental protection; their claims have implications for regulation (and life) in general.[22] Arrow and Fisher imagine that the question is whether to preserve a virgin redwood forest for wilderness recreation or instead to open it to clear-cut logging. Assume that if the development option is chosen, the destruction of the forest is effectively irreversible. Arrow and Fisher argue that it matters whether the authorities cannot yet assess the costs or benefits of a proposed development. If development produces "some irreversible transformation of the environment, hence a loss in perpetuity of the benefits from preservation," then it is worth paying something to wait to acquire the missing information. Their suggestion is that "the expected benefits of an irreversible decision should be adjusted to reflect the loss of options it entails."[23]

Fisher has generalized this argument to suggest that "[w]here a decision problem is characterized by (1) uncertainty about future costs and benefits of the alternatives, (2) prospects for resolving or reducing the uncertainty with the passage of time, and (3) irreversibility of one or more of the alternatives, an extra value, an option value, properly attaches to the reversible alternative(s)."[24] The intuition here is both straightforward and appealing: More steps should be taken to prevent harms that are effectively final than to prevent those that can be reversed at some cost. If an irreversible harm is on one side and a reversible one on the other, and if decision makers are uncertain[25] about future costs and benefits of precautions, an understanding of option value suggests that it is worthwhile to spend a certain amount to preserve future flexibility, by paying a premium to avoid the irreversible harm.

Writing in 2004, Judge Richard Posner made a point of this sort as a justification for taking aggressive steps to combat climate change.[26] Posner acknowledged that the size of the threat of climate change was disputed (as it certainly was in 2004, and remains today), and hence it is tempting to wait to regulate until we have more information. But there is a serious problem with waiting, which is "the practically irreversible effect of greenhouse-gas emissions on the atmospheric concentration of those gases."[27] Thus Posner reasoned that making aggressive "cuts now can be thought of as purchasing an option to enable global warming to be stopped or slowed at some future time at a lower cost."[28] The reduction in cost, as a result of current steps, could result from lowering current emissions or simply from increasing the rate of technological innovations that make pollution reduction less costly in the future. Posner concluded that the option approach makes sense for other catastrophic risks as well, including those associated with genetically modified crops.

The general point here is that, as in the stock market, those involved in environmental protection and regulation generally are trying to project a stream of good and bad effects over time. The ability to project the stream of effects will improve, and hence much can be gained from being able to make the decision later in time rather than earlier. If a better decision can be made in the future, then there is a value to putting the decision off to a later date, which may make it necessary to freeze the status quo, perhaps through costly regulation now. The key point is that uncertainty and irreversibility should lead to a sequential decision-making process. If better information will emerge, regulators might seek an approach that preserves greater flexibility, at least if that approach is not too costly. The extent of the appropriate "irreversibility premium" depends on the details.

## Seriousness and Sunk Costs

Even under this account, the idea of irreversibility remains ambiguous. Let us consider two possible interpretations. Under the first, an effect is irreversible when restoration to the status quo is impossible or at best extremely difficult, at least on a relevant timescale. For example, the "decision not to preserve a rich reservoir of biodiversity such as the 60-million-year-old Korup forest in Nigeria is irreversible. The alteration or destruction of a unique asset of this type has an awesome finality."[29] If this is the appropriate interpretation of irreversibility, then it is a part of the broader concern of seriousness ("awesome finality"). A second interpretation, standard in the economic literature on options, sees irreversibility in terms of sunk costs. The two interpretations lead to different understandings of the problem of irreversibility and the Irreversible Harm Precautionary Principle.

Under the first interpretation, the question is whether a clear line separates the reversible from the irreversible.[30] Perhaps we have a continuum, not a dichotomy. The question is not whether some effect can be reversed, but instead at what cost. Note that areas that have been developed, or otherwise harmed, can often be returned to their original state, even if at considerable expense. Even lost forests can be restored. But sometimes the cost is high, even prohibitive, and sometimes restoration is literally impossible. Consider in this regard the mortality effects of certain environmental harms. If air pollution would kill 200 people a year, or if climate change would produce tens of thousands of deaths in India, those losses cannot be recovered. Even biological changes in the human body may not be reversible (whether or not they are associated with immediate or long-term harm). Some kinds of air pollution induce changes that endure for decades. In all of these cases, irreversibility is simply an aspect of seriousness. If 200 people will die from certain levels of pollution, the harm is more serious than if 200 people would merely get sick. If air pollution induces biological changes, everything depends on the magnitude of the harm associated with those changes.

At first glance, these points do not create a serious problem for the Irreversible Harm Precautionary Principle. The extent of the precautions should depend on the size of the harms and the cost and burden associated with preventing or (if possible) reversing those harms. If climate change cannot be reversed at all, we should take more aggressive precautions than we would if it can be reversed only at great expense, monetary or otherwise—and if it can be reversed only at great expense, we would take more precautions than we would if it would be easy to reverse it.

But there is a more severe conceptual difficulty, which is that *whether a particular act is "irreversible" depends on how it is characterized.* Any death, of any living creature, is irreversible, and what is true for living creatures is true for rocks and refrigerators too; if these are destroyed, they are destroyed forever. And because time is linear, every decision is, in an intelligible sense, irreversible. If a couple goes on vacation in Greece in July of a certain year, that decision cannot be reversed, and what else might have been done at that time will have been permanently lost. If the government builds a new highway in upstate New York in May, that particular decision will be irreversible; nothing else will be done with that land in May, even though the highway can be later replaced or eliminated. This is the sense in which "irreversibility" depends on how the underlying act is characterized. If we characterize it narrowly, to be and to do precisely what it is and does, any act is irreversible by definition.

Environmentalists who are concerned about irreversibility have something far more particular in mind. They mean something like a large-scale alteration in environmental conditions—one that imposes permanent, or nearly permanent, changes in those conditions. It should be clear that irreversibility in this sense is not a sufficient reason for a highly precautionary approach. At a minimum, the irreversible change has to be for the worse, and it must also rise to a certain level of magnitude. A truly minuscule change in the global temperature, even if permanent, would not justify expensive precautions if it is benign or if it imposes little in the way of harm. For this reason, it is tempting to understand the idea of irreversibility, for environmental purposes, as inseparable from that of seriousness. A loss of a wisdom tooth is irreversible, but not a reason for particular precautions on behalf of wisdom teeth; a loss of an extremely small forest, with no wildlife, hardly justifies a special principle, even if that loss cannot be reversed. A loss of a large forest, with a lot of wildlife, is a very different matter.

At first glance, then, irreversibility matters only because of its connection with the magnitude of the harm; irreversibility operates as a kind of amplifier. In law, an illuminating comparison might be made with the idea that courts will refuse to issue a preliminary injunction unless the plaintiff can show that there is a likelihood of an "irreparable harm" if the injunction is not granted.[31] Irreparability is not a sufficient condition for granting the injunction; the harm must be serious as well as irreparable. And if irreversibility in environmental protection is to be analyzed in the same way, then an Irreversible Harm Precautionary Principle is really part of a Catastrophic Harm Precautionary Principle, or at least a Significant Harm Precautionary Principle.

If so, the Irreversible Harm Precautionary Principle is important and must be taken into account, but it is not especially distinctive. The principle is also vulnerable, some of the time, to the same objections that apply to the Precautionary Principle as a whole. As we shall see, significant and even irreversible harms may well be on all sides of risk-related problems, and a focus on one set of risks will give rise to others—perhaps environmental risks as well.

Analysts of real options understand the idea of irreversibility in a different way.[32] Irreversible investments are sunk costs—those that cannot be recovered. Examples include expenditures on advertising and marketing, or even capital investments designed to improve the performance of a factory. In fact, the purchase of motor vehicles, computers, and office equipment is not fully reversible, because the purchase cost is usually significantly higher than resale value. Examples of reversible investments include the opening of bank accounts and the purchase of bonds. The problem with an investment that is irreversible is that those who make it relinquish "the possibility of waiting for new information that might affect the desirability or timing of the expenditure, and this lost option value is an opportunity cost that must be included as part of the investment."[33]

Many people agree that we should characterize as irreversible harms those environmental effects that are both serious and extremely expensive and time-consuming to reverse. This is the understanding that leads Posner and others to argue for the purchase of an "option" to slow down climate change at a lower rate in the future. Immediate adoption of a policy produces a "sunk benefit." The argument is correct, but it must be added that *irreversibility, in this sense, might well lie on all sides.*[34] Regulation that reduces one (irreversible) environmental risk might increase another such risk.

In some nations, efforts to reduce climate change and other dangers associated with fossil fuels may lead to increased dependence on nuclear power, which threatens to produce irreversible harms of its own; in China, for example, nuclear energy has sometimes been defended as a way of combating climate change. As with the Precautionary Principle in general, so with the Irreversible Harm Precautionary Principle in particular: Measures that the principle requires, on grounds of irreversible harm, might well be prohibited on exactly those grounds. And there is a more general point. If steps are taken to reduce greenhouse gas emissions, capital costs will be incurred, and they cannot be recouped. Sunk costs are a familiar feature of environmental regulation, in the form of mandates that require technological change. We may well be dealing, then, with irreversibilities, not irreversibility.[35]

For many environmental problems, this point complicates the application of the Irreversible Harm Precautionary Principle. As Fisher writes of climate change, "it is not clear whether the conditions of the problem imply that investment in control ought to be slowed or reduced, while waiting for information needed to make a better decision, or that investment should come sooner to preserve the option to protect ourselves from impacts that may be revealed in the future as serious or even catastrophic."[36] It is for this reason that, unlike Judge Posner, some observers have concluded that the existence of uncertainty and irreversibility argues for *less*, not more, current investments in reducing greenhouse gas emissions. Those investments may themselves turn out to be irreversible. Everything depends on the likelihood and magnitude of the losses on all sides.

Judge Posner emphasizes the cumulative effect of emissions on atmospheric concentrations of carbon dioxide.[37] Because of that cumulative effect, a steady or even declining rate of emissions will still cause concentrations to increase. He also notes that it may be much harder and more expensive to slow climate change in the future than in the present—a point that comes close to the understanding of irreversibility in the economic literature. But a full analysis of irreversibility must also attend to the irreversible losses associated with greenhouse gas *reductions*. As Pindyck puts it:[38]

It has been long understood that environmental damage can be irreversible, which can lead to a more "conservationist" policy than would be optimal otherwise. Thanks to Joni Mitchell, even non-economists know that if we "pave paradise and put up a parking lot," paradise may be gone forever. And because the value of paradise to future generations is uncertain, the benefit from protecting it today should include an option value, which pushes the cost-benefit calculation towards protection. But there is a second kind of irreversibility that works in the opposite direction: Protecting paradise over the years to come imposes sunk costs on society. If paradise includes clean air and water, protecting it could imply sunk cost investments in abatement equipment, and an ongoing flow of sunk costs for more expensive production processes. This kind of irreversibility would lead to policies that are less "conservationist" than they would be otherwise.

Climate change in particular involves competing irreversibilities. Because $CO_2$ remains in the atmosphere for centuries, the environmental damage from $CO_2$ emissions is effectively irreversible, which strengthens the arguments for acting early and aggressively. But reducing $CO_2$ emissions requires the imposition of sunk costs, in the form of irreversible expenditures, which argues against early and aggressive actions.

Nothing said here supports the implausible view that the right approach to climate change is adequately captured in the area of "wait and learn." In light of the science, immediate action is an excellent idea, even if we dispute its magnitude and its form. "Wait and learn" must itself be subject to a cost-benefit test; it makes most sense if we lose very little when we defer investments while waiting to obtain more information about their benefits. If a great deal is likely to be lost by deferring such investments, then we should not wait and learn; and there is good reason to believe that the irreversible losses associated with climate change do indeed justify the irreversible losses associated with greater investments in emissions reductions. My conclusion is that if irreversibility is defined in standard economic terms, pointing to the value of preserving flexibility for an uncertain future, it provides a distinctive and plausible understanding of the Irreversible Harm Precautionary Principle. This understanding also helps explain some of the most important functions of NEPA.

## Irreversibility and Incommensurability

The discussion thus far misses something important. When people say that the loss of a pristine area or of a species is irreversible, they do not merely mean that the loss is grave and that it takes a lot to provide adequate compensation. They mean that what is lost is *incommensurable*—that it is qualitatively distinctive, and that when we lose it, we lose something that is unique.

The central claim here is that human goods are diverse and that we do violence to our considered judgments about them when we line them up along a single metric.[39] Suppose, for example, that a species of tigers or elephants is lost. People do not value an endangered species in the same way that they value money; it is not as if a species, a beach, a friendship, or a child is indistinguishable from specified monetary sums. If we see species, beaches, friendships, and children as equivalent to one another, or to some amount of money, we will have an odd and even unrecognizable understanding of all of these things. When people object to the loss of a species or a beach and contend that the loss is irreversible, they mean to point to its permanence and to the fact that what has been lost is not valued in the same way, or valued along the same metric, as money.

This claim should not be confused. Of course, people are willing to make trade-offs among qualitatively diverse goods, and they do so all the time. We will pay a certain amount, and no more, to protect members of an endangered species or to visit the beach, or to help preserve it in a pristine state;

we will not pay an infinite sum to see our friends, or even to maintain our friendships; we will take some precautions, but not others, to protect our children. The emphasis on incommensurability is not meant to deny that trade-offs are made. The point is only that the relevant goods are not the same. It follows that when a loss is deemed irreversible, it is because it is qualitatively distinctive and not fungible with other human goods. Many of those who are concerned about irreversible harms intend to stress this point.

This claim offers a distinctive understanding of what is meant by the idea of irreversibility. When losses are said to be irreversible, it is often because of the uniqueness of what is lost. The need for trade-offs remains important. A single person is incommensurable with money and with other things that matter, but we do not attempt to drive risks of death down to zero. The claim about irreversibility does not mean that we should devote an infinite amount, or any particular amount, to prevent an incommensurable loss. What is gained by an understanding of incommensurability is a more vivid appreciation of why certain losses cannot be dismissed as mere "costs."

An Irreversible Harm Precautionary Principle, used in private decisions or democratic arenas, might be implemented with a recognition of the qualitative distinctness of many losses—including losses that affect future generations. Here too, however, it is important to see that precautionary steps may themselves impose incommensurable losses, not merely monetary ones. Recall, for example, that environmental protection of one sort may create environmental problems of another sort. If the diverse nature of social goods is to play a part in the implementation of an Irreversible Harm Precautionary Principle, it must attend to the fact that diverse goods may be on all sides.

## Qualifications

The arguments for an Irreversible Harm Precautionary Principle, along with an understanding of its limitations, are now in place. We lack any kind of algorithm for implementing that principle. But we should be able to agree that when a harm is irreversible in the sense that it is very costly or impossible to make restoration, special precautions may be justified; that it often makes sense to "buy" an option to preserve future flexibility; and that the loss of cherished and qualitatively distinctive goods deserves particular attention. But there are three important qualifications, involving the idea of optimal delay, distributional considerations, and what I shall call precommitment value. Let us briefly explore each of these.

### Irreversibilities and Optimal Delay

The general notion of optimal delay provides important countervailing considerations. Future generations will almost certainly be both wealthier and more knowledgeable than the current generation. For this reason, they will be in a far better position, and possibly an unimaginably better position, to handle environmental problems that materialize in their time. Thomas Schelling urges that the nearly inevitable increase in wealth over time means that it "makes no sense to make current generations 'pay' for the problems of future generations."[40] Why should the relatively poor present transfer its limited resources to benefit the future, which is likely to be relatively rich? There is another problem. The problem of climate change might turn out to be unique, but expensive investments in precautions—including greenhouse gas reductions—may turn out to diminish available resources for future generations, leaving them with less to use to control the damage that actually occurs.

The argument for "wait and learn" is strengthened by these points. But any such argument must also take account of the incontrovertible fact that waiting simultaneously threatens to diminish the flexibility of future decision makers, and perhaps severely. Compare the loss of endangered species; because the loss is permanent, we have to be careful about delaying precautionary measures designed to ensure their continued existence.

## Irreversibilities, Distribution, and the Least Well-Off

At first glance, an Irreversible Harm Precautionary Principle might seem to be especially beneficial to disadvantaged people.[41] In the context of climate change, aggressive precautions are projected to help poor countries more than rich ones, partly because rich nations are able to spend more on adaptation and resilience, and partly because they are much less dependent on agriculture. Air pollution often most hurts people at the bottom of the economic ladder. Nonetheless, there is no simple connection between distributional goals and an emphasis on irreversible harms. Some of the risks associated with genetic modification of food are irreversible, but its benefits might be largest in poor nations. In the context of climate change, such nations might find it especially difficult to pay for expensive regulation. Whenever prices are raised, people without much money will find it hardest to pay the bills.

In short, the analysis of distributional goals must be undertaken separately from the analysis of irreversibility. Sometimes we will hurt the least well-off, rather than help them, if we buy an option to preserve our own flexibility. The cost of the option might be paid mostly by those who can least afford it.

## Precommitment Value

I have emphasized the value of preserving our flexibility. But in some domains, future flexibility is undesirable, and individuals and societies are willing to pay a great deal to eliminate it. The tale of Ulysses and the Sirens is perhaps the most familiar example, and the idea of precommitment has many applications. Constitutions can be seen as precommitment devices, by which we relinquish our flexibility in order to be governed by firm rules. With respect to terrorism, we might do best if we commit ourselves to taking certain courses of action if we are attacked—the precommitment creates deterrence.

In the environmental context, regulators might be willing to pay for precommitment strategies that will operate as a constraint on any number of problems, including interest-group power, myopia, weakness of will, and cognitive biases. Indeed, the conventional Precautionary Principle, understood to place a thumb on the scales in favor of environmental protection, might be explained in these terms. Perhaps the principle can be understood not as an effort to preserve flexibility, which can be bad, but on the contrary as an effort to ensure a commitment to a course of action that will protect the environment.

The difficulty for any such explanation should now be familiar: Any precommitment strategy may give rise to serious problems, including environmental problems, for which a precommitment strategy might also be justified. It is nonetheless important to see that option value is sometimes paralleled by "precommitment value," for which regulators might be willing to spend a great deal.

# Conclusion

In both ordinary life and public policy, people must often make decisions without important information. Taking a new job is an example; so is moving to a new city; so is starting a romance or getting married. For the COVID-19 pandemic, leaders had to make a large number of decisions, sometimes in the relative dark. For climate change, there is so much that we do not know. In any particular year, the risk of a financial meltdown, or a serious terrorist attack, might be surrounded by question marks. Or suppose that the issue is whether to undertake some reform of the police force, in a way that reduces the risk of police violence while potentially reducing the ability of police officers to protect people against private crime. Some of the key questions may not have clear answers.

For some of these issues, it might be tempting to "wait and learn," but doing that might create serious risks. At the same time, a stab in the dark is not a good idea. So too, the general idea of "better safe than sorry" is unhelpful when risks to safety and health can be found from action, inaction, and everything in between. Consider, for example, the fact that the most aggressive responses to COVID-19, imposing something like a shutdown, can create severe economic distress (which is not good for people's physical health) and also an increase in mental health problems. Health-health trade-offs might be inescapable. By contrast, breakeven analysis might turn out to solve the problem: If we know the lower bound or the upper bound for benefits, we might know what costs it does and does not make sense to incur.

A great deal of work explores the question whether people should follow the maximin principle under circumstances of uncertainty.[1] Some of this work draws on people's intuitions in a way that illuminates actual beliefs but may tell us little about what rationality requires.[2] Other work is highly formal,[3] adopting certain axioms and seeing whether the maximin principle violates them. The results of this work are not conclusive. Certainly, the maximin principle cannot be rejected as a candidate for rational choice under Knightian uncertainty.

I will rest content with three general suggestions. *First*: As we have seen, the maximin principle is sometimes justified by standard cost-benefit analysis. If some potential outcomes are genuinely catastrophic and not highly improbable, eliminating them might be the approach that maximizes net benefits. Even if such outcomes are highly improbable (say, 1 in 10,000), the same conclusion might be the right one if the expected value of precautions outweighs their expected cost.

*Second*: In the face of fat tails (suggesting a higher-than-normal risk of catastrophe, as in "ruin problems"), there may be a good argument for the maximin principle, again depending on the numbers (and on what is known and what is unknown). This is so without and especially with risk aversion. Nordhaus puts it this way: "in the presence of both fat-tailed uncertain outcomes and strong risk aversion, we cannot rely upon our standard tools of expected utility analysis. The reason is that the probability of extreme and catastrophic events does not decline sufficiently rapidly to compensate for our aversion to encountering these catastrophic events."[4]

*Third*: Uncertainty is real. Sometimes regulators lack information about probabilities. In deciding whether to follow the maximin principle under circumstances of Knightian uncertainty, or something close to it (such as bounded uncertainty), a great deal should turn on two questions: (a) How bad is the worst-case scenario, compared to other bad outcomes? (b) What, exactly, is lost by choosing the maximin principle? Of course, it is possible that choosers, including regulators, will lack the information that would enable them to answer these questions. But (and this is the central point) in the regulatory context, answers to both (a) and (b) may well be possible *even if it is not possible to assign probabilities to the various outcomes with any confidence*. By emphasizing the relative badness of the worst-case scenario, and the magnitude of the loss from trying to eliminate it, I am attempting to build on the Rawls/Gardiner suggestion that maximin is the preferred decision rule when little is lost from following it.

To see the relevance of the two questions, suppose that you are choosing between two options. The first has a best-case outcome of 10 and a worst-case outcome of −5. The second has a best-case outcome of 15 and a worst-case outcome of −6. It is impossible to assign probabilities to the various outcomes. Maximin would favor the first option, to avoid the worse worst-case outcome (which is −6); but to justify that choice, we have to know something about the *meaning* of the differences between 10 and 15 on the one hand and −5 and −6 on the other. If 15 is much better than 10, and if the difference between −5 and −6 is a matter of relative indifference, then the choice of the first option is hardly mandated. But if the difference between −5 and −6 greatly matters—if it is a matter of life and death—then the maximin principle is much more attractive.

Consider a regulatory analogue. Suppose that as compared with a ban, allowing self-driving vehicles would have a best-case outcome of $2 billion in annual net benefits and a worst-case outcome of −$10 million in annual net benefits. Suppose that we cannot assign probabilities to the various outcomes. Under the maximin principle, we should ban self-driving vehicles. But if the net loss of $10 million is not a big deal, we might reject the maximin principle. Of course, we could vary the numbers in such a way as to make the maximin principle much more attractive.

These points suggest the possibility of a (rough) cost-benefit analysis of whether to follow the maximin principle under conditions of both risk and uncertainty.[5] Sometimes the worst case is the worst by far, and sometimes we lose relatively little by choosing the maximin principle. It is typically thought necessary to assign probabilities in order to engage in cost-benefit balancing; without an understanding of probabilities, such balancing might not seem able to get off the ground. But a crude version of cost-benefit balancing is possible even without reliable information about probability. For the balancing exercise to work, of course, it must be possible to produce cardinal rankings among the outcomes—that is, it must be possible to rank them not merely in terms of their badness but also in at least rough terms of how much worse each is than the less-bad others. That approach will not work if cardinal rankings are not feasible—as might be the case if (for example) it is not easy to compare the catastrophic loss from a pandemic with the catastrophic loss from huge expenditures on efforts to control a pandemic. Much of the time, however, cardinal rankings are possible in the regulatory context.

Here is a simpler way to put the point. It is often assumed that to undertake cost-benefit analysis, it is necessary to identify potential outcomes and to assign probabilities, producing an assessment of expected value. But in some cases, sensible rules of thumb can be adopted without assigning probabilities. If, for example, one option has a large downside but no substantial upside, it can be rejected in favor of one that lacks that downside but that has a roughly equivalent upside.

To appreciate the need for some kind of analysis of the effects of following the maximin principle, imagine an individual or society lacking the information that would permit the assignment of probabilities to a series of hazards with catastrophic outcomes; suppose that the number of hazards is 10, or 20, or 1,000. Suppose too that such an individual or society is able to assign probabilities (ranging from 1% to 90%) to an equivalent number of *other* hazards, with outcomes that range from bad to extremely bad, but never catastrophic. Suppose, finally, that every one of these hazards can be eliminated at a cost—a cost that is high but that would not inflict harms that count as extremely bad or catastrophic. The maximin principle suggests that our individual or society should spend a great deal to eliminate each of the 10, or 20, or 1,000 potentially catastrophic hazards. But once that amount is spent on even one of those hazards, there might be nothing left to combat the extremely bad hazards, even those with a 90% chance of occurring. We could even imagine that a poorly informed individual or society would be condemned to real poverty and distress or even worse, merely by virtue of following maximin. In these circumstances, the maximin principle runs into obvious objections.

This suggestion is broadly consistent with the empirical finding that when asked to decide on the distribution of goods and services, most people reject the two most widely discussed principles in the philosophical literature: average utility, favored by Harsanyi, and Rawls's difference principle (justified, as we have seen, by reference to the maximin principle, and allowing inequalities only if they work to the advantage of the least well-off).[6] Instead, people choose average utility with a floor constraint—that is, they favor an approach that maximizes overall well-being, but subject to the constraint that no member of society may fall below a decent minimum.[7] Insisting on an absolute welfare minimum to all, they maximize over that floor. They reject average utility; they also reject maximin, but their aversion to especially bad outcomes leads them to a pragmatic threshold in the form of the floor.

So too, very plausibly, in the context of precautions against risks. A sensible individual, or society, would not always choose maximin under circumstances of risk or uncertainty. Everything depends on what is lost, and what is gained, by eliminating the worst-case scenario; and much of the time, available information makes it possible to answer that question, at least in general terms.

Irreversibility also matters, in the sense that it makes sense to pay a premium to maintain options. When we do not know costs and benefits, when we will learn about them over time, and when a loss is irreversible, policymakers should be willing to pay something to maintain flexibility for the future. The basic intuition is familiar in private life—consider a decision to move, to marry, or to take a new job. The problem of climate change involves potentially irreversible losses (on both sides).

If we apply these various points, we could easily imagine an amendment to OMB Circular A-4 that takes the following form:[8]

> In general, it is appropriate to focus on costs and benefits, calculated by reference to the expected value of various options. Thus, your analysis should include two fundamental components: a quantitative analysis characterizing the probabilities of the relevant outcomes and an assignment of economic value to the projected outcomes. It is essential that both parts be conceptually consistent. It is also essential that both parts include any irreversible losses. In particular, the quantitative analysis should be conducted in a way that permits it to be applied within the more general analytical framework of benefit-cost analysis. If one or another outcome is potentially catastrophic (a "worst case"), it might make sense to eliminate it, if the analysis shows that doing so maximizes

net benefits. In considering potential catastrophe, you should consider the possibility of "fat tails," which arise when the probability of extreme negative outcomes is unusually high. Complex systems may be especially prone to fat tails.

In some cases, it may not be feasible to come up with probability distributions. If so, your analysis should be as complete as the available evidence permits. For example, it might include a specification of lower and upper bounds, with a qualitative analysis of their respective likelihoods (to the extent possible). Breakeven analysis might prove helpful here. In special circumstances, you might consider avoiding the worst-case scenario and thus following the maximin principle, which calls for eliminating the worst of the worst cases. The strongest cases for following that rule would involve three factors: (1) Knightian uncertainty, understood as an inability to assign probabilities to various options; (2) catastrophic or grave consequences from one option, but not from other options; and (3) low or relatively low costs, or low or relatively low benefits foregone, as a result of choosing the option that avoids the worst-case scenario. In situations of uncertainty, more difficult cases, in which (for example) the costs of avoiding the worst-case scenario are very high, might also warrant use of the maximin principle if (for example) the worst-case scenario is genuinely catastrophic. In some cases, it might make sense to delay aggressive regulation in the face of uncertainty, while learning occurs about the relevant probabilities.

For prudent regulators attempting to proceed in the midst of important epistemic gaps, the maximin principle makes most sense when the worst-case scenario under one course of action is much worse than the worst-case scenario under the alternative course of action, when there are no huge disparities in gains from either option, and when the choice of maximin does not result in extremely significant losses. Variations on this case are easy to imagine. For example, use of the maximin principle might prove exceptionally costly, in which case the argument on its behalf becomes less compelling, and regulators face harder challenges.

It is also important for prudent regulators to focus on the best-case scenarios, which may promise miracles;[9] that possibility provides an important cautionary note about efforts to eliminate risks, including those posed by new technologies. Human history is full of cases in which such technologies caused grave concern and in which the maximin approach would have been devastating; consider automobiles, airplanes, computers, cell phones, and medicines of multiple sorts. Taken very seriously, the maximin approach is at war with innovation, and that is not a good war to wage.

Much of the discussion here has been based on stylized problems with specific numbers, abstracting from the more disorderly world of policymaking. My hope is that the stylized problems reveal the importance of focusing on the expected value of options, with the belief that options with the highest such values are generally best. With respect to climate change and COVID-19, it is true that we might insist on a degree of risk aversion, so long as its price is not too high. It is also true that we need to know a fair bit to know how to determine expected value—not only to answer questions of science and economics, but also to think well about human welfare. Distributional issues matter.[10] If poor people or the most disadvantaged are especially vulnerable, conscientious policymakers ought to be especially responsive.[11]

But my main goal lies elsewhere. Usually it is a mistake to adopt the maximin principle or anything close to it, because doing so would make people's lives worse and often much worse. The most aggressive responses to risks, including catastrophic risks, can cause real suffering and give rise to catastrophic risks of their own. We also need to focus on miracles, not only on catastrophes, and excessive precautions may prevent miracles. But in identifiable cases, aggressive responses, embodying something like the maximin principle, are not mistakes at all. The easiest of such cases involve catastrophic outcomes with relatively high probabilities—as in the case of the COVID-19 pandemic of 2020. Nearly as easy are cases that involve catastrophic outcomes with relatively low probabilities—as in the case of financial crises. The hardest cases, and the most interesting, involve catastrophic outcomes with unknown probabilities.

In such cases, there is a strong argument for adopting the maximin principle when the cost of doing so is zero or very low; in those circumstances, the Rawls/Gardiner argument for precautions is convincing. When the cost is very high, the argument for doing so naturally weakens. Limited resources might be devoted to a wide range of problems, including those for which the known probability of catastrophe is high. With respect to climate change, here is a helpful summary from Pindyck:[12]

We need to assess as best we can the probability distributions for climate outcomes and their impact, with an emphasis on the more extreme outcomes. We also need to better understand the cost of shifting those distributions, that is, the cost of "climate insurance." And all of this needs to be done in the context of budget constraints and other societal needs, including schools, highways, and defense, as well as the cost of "insurance" against other potential catastrophes.

In the hardest and most intriguing cases, it is not possible to defend any simple rule. Some kind of judgment must be made. Nothing in decision theory can specify that judgment. But in the face of unknown probabilities of catastrophe for which "wait and learn" is clearly imprudent, it is reasonable to take strong protective measures, whether the problem involves COVID-19, climate change, or the kinds of dangers that each of us faces in ordinary life. Those measures will enable us to sleep better at night. And if we end up buying too much insurance, well, so be it.

# ACKNOWLEDGMENTS

Special thanks to William Nordhaus and Robert Pindyck for careful readings and for valuable comments and suggestions; I am acutely aware that I have not responded adequately. Thanks too to Sendhil Mullainathan for greatly illuminating discussions. I am grateful to Tyler Cowen, Annie Duke, and Eric Posner for superb comments on an earlier draft and to Lia Cattaneo and Dinis Cheian for extraordinary research assistance. Thanks to Sarah Chalfant, my agent, for support and help of multiple kinds. My editor, Clara Platter, provided terrific guidance and suggestions. I am also grateful to three anonymous reviewers for valuable suggestions.

I have been working on these topics for many years. Parts of this book draw on previous work, including Cass R. Sunstein, *Beyond the Precautionary Principle*, 151 U. PA. L. REV 1003 (2003), and Cass R. Sunstein, *Irreversible and Catastrophic*, 91 CORNELL L. REV. 841 (2006), the latter of which made its way into Cass R. Sunstein, *Worst-Case Scenarios* (2007), which can be seen as a forerunner of this book. My most relevant and recent discussion is Cass R. Sunstein, *Maximin*, 37 YALE J. REG. 940 (2020); I am most grateful for permission to draw on that discussion here.

# APPENDIX A

**March 11, 2011**

Memorandum for the Heads of Executive Departments and Agencies

FROM: John P. Holdren
Assistant to the President for Science and Technology
Director, Office of Science and Technology Policy
Cass R. Sunstein
Administrator, Office of Information and Regulatory Affairs
Office of Management and Budget
Islam A. Siddiqui
Chief Agricultural Negotiator
United States Trade Representative
SUBJECT: Principles for Regulation and Oversight of Emerging Technologies

Innovation with respect to emerging technologies—such as nano-technology, synthetic biology, and genetic engineering, among others—requires not only coordinated research and development but also appropriate and balanced oversight. The White House Emerging Technologies Interagency Policy Coordination Committee (ETIPC) has developed the following broad principles, consistent

with Executive Order 13563, to guide the development and implementation of policies for oversight of emerging technologies at the
agency level.

We share a fundamental desire for regulation and oversight that
ensure the fulfillment of legitimate objectives such as the protection
of safety, health, and the environment. Regulation and oversight
should avoid unjustifiably inhibiting innovation, stigmatizing new
technologies, or creating trade barriers.

To advance these goals, the following principles, consistent with
Executive Order 13563 and discussed and approved by the ETIPC,
should be respected to the extent permitted by law:

Scientific Integrity: Federal regulation and oversight of emerging technologies should be based on the best available scientific
evidence. Adequate information should be sought and developed,
and new knowledge should be taken into account when it becomes
available. To the extent feasible, purely scientific judgments should
be separated from judgments of policy.

Public Participation: To the extent feasible and subject to valid
constraints (involving, for example, national security and con-
fidential business information), relevant information should be
developed with ample opportunities for stakeholder involvement
and public participation. Public participation is important for
promoting accountability, for improving decisions, for increasing trust, and for ensuring that officials have access to widely
dispersed information.

Communication: The Federal Government should actively communicate information to the public regarding the potential benefits and risks associated with new technologies.

Benefits and costs: Federal regulation and oversight of emerging technologies should be based on an awareness of the potential benefits and the potential costs of such regulation and oversight, including recognition of the role of limited information and risk in decision making.

Flexibility: To the extent practicable, Federal regulation and oversight should provide sufficient flexibility to accommodate new evidence and learning and to take into account the evolving nature of information related to emerging technologies and their applications.

Risk Assessment and Risk Management: Risk assessment should be distinguished from risk management. The Federal Government should strive to reach an appropriate level of consistency in risk assessment and risk management across various agencies and offices and across various technologies. Federally mandated risk management actions should be appropriate to, and commensurate with, the degree of risk identified in an assessment.

Coordination: Federal agencies should seek to coordinate with one another, with state authorities, and with stakeholders to address the breadth of issues, including health and safety, economic, environmental, and ethical issues (where applicable) associated with the commercialization of an emerging technology, in an effort to craft a coherent approach. There should be a clear recognition of the statutory limitations of each Federal and state agency and an effort to defer to appropriate entities when attempting to address the breadth of issues.

International Cooperation: The Federal Government should encourage coordinated and collaborative research across the international community. It should clearly communicate the regulatory approaches and understanding of the United States to other nations. It should promote informed choices and both sharing and development of relevant data, particularly with respect to the benefits and costs of regulation and oversight. The Federal Government should participate in the development of international standards, consistent with U.S. law and guidance (e.g., the National Technology Transfer and Advancement Act and OMB Circular A-119). When appropriate, international approaches should be coordinated as far in advance as possible, to help ensure that such approaches are consistent with these principles.

Regulation: The Federal Government should adhere to Executive Order 13563 and, consistent with that Executive Order, the following principles, to the extent permitted by law, when regulating emerging technologies:

- Decisions should be based on the best reasonably obtainable scientific, technical, economic, and other information, within the boundaries of the authorities and mandates of each agency;
- Regulations should be developed with a firm commitment to fair notice and to public participation;

- The benefits of regulation should justify the costs (to the extent permitted by law and recognizing the relevance of uncertainty and the limits of quantification and monetary equivalents);

- Where possible, regulatory approaches should promote innovation while also advancing regulatory objectives, such as protection of health, the environment, and safety;

- When no significant oversight issue based on a sufficiently distinguishing attribute of the technology or the relevant application can be identified, agencies should consider the option not to regulate;

- Where possible, regulatory approaches should be performance-based and provide predictability and flexibility in the face of fresh evidence and evolving information; and

- Regulatory approaches shall comply with established requirements and guidance . . .

# APPENDIX B

Circular A-4

**September 17, 2003**

. . .

Treatment of Uncertainty

The precise consequences (benefits and costs) of regulatory options are not always known for certain, but the probability of their occurrence can often be developed. The important uncertainties connected with your regulatory decisions need to be analyzed and presented as part of the overall regulatory analysis. You should begin your analysis of uncertainty at the earliest possible stage in developing your analysis. You should consider both the statistical variability of key elements underlying the estimates of benefits and costs (for example, the expected change in the distribution of automobile accidents that might result from a change in automobile safety standards) and the incomplete knowledge about the relevant relationships (for example, the uncertain knowledge of how some economic activities might affect future climate change).* By assess-

*In some contexts, the word "variability" is used as a synonym for statistical variation that can be described by a theoretically valid distribution function, whereas "uncertainty" refers to a more fundamental lack of knowledge. Throughout this discussion, we use the term "uncertainty" to refer to both concepts.

ing the sources of uncertainty and the way in which benefit and cost estimates may be affected under plausible assumptions, you can shape your analysis to inform decision makers and the public about the effects and the uncertainties of alternative regulatory actions.

The treatment of uncertainty must be guided by the same principles of full disclosure and transparency that apply to other elements of your regulatory analysis. Your analysis should be credible, objective, realistic, and scientifically balanced.* Any data and models that you use to analyze uncertainty should be fully identified. You should also discuss the quality of the available data used. Inferences and assumptions used in your analysis should be identified, and your analytical choices should be explicitly evaluated and adequately justified. In your presentation, you should delineate the strengths of your analysis along with any uncertainties about its conclusions. Your presentation should also explain how your analytical choices have affected your results.

In some cases, the level of scientific uncertainty may be so large that you can only present discrete alternative scenarios without assessing the relative likelihood of each scenario quantitatively. For instance, in assessing the potential outcomes of an environmental effect, there may be a limited number of scientific studies with strongly divergent results. In such cases, you might present results from a range of plausible scenarios, together with any available

*When disseminating information, agencies should follow their own information quality guidelines, issued in conformance with the OMB government-wide guidelines (67 FR 8452, February 22, 2002).

information that might help in qualitatively determining which scenario is most likely to occur.

When uncertainty has significant effects on the final conclusion about net benefits, your agency should consider additional research prior to rulemaking. The costs of being wrong may outweigh the benefits of a faster decision. This is true especially for cases with irreversible or large upfront investments. If your agency decides to proceed with rulemaking, you should explain why the costs of developing additional information—including any harm from delay in public protection—exceed the value of that information.

For example, when the uncertainty is due to a lack of data, you might consider deferring the decision, as an explicit regulatory alternative, pending further study to obtain sufficient data.* Delaying a decision will also have costs, as will further efforts at data gathering and analysis. You will need to weigh the benefits of delay against these costs in making your decision. Formal tools for assessing the value of additional information are now well developed in the applied decision sciences and can be used to help resolve this type of complex regulatory question.

"Real options" methods have also formalized the valuation of the added flexibility inherent in delaying a decision. As long as taking time will lower uncertainty, either passively or actively through an investment in information gathering, and some costs are irreversible, such as the potential costs of a sunk investment, a benefit can

*Clemen RT (1996), *Making Hard Decisions: An Introduction to Decision Analysis*, second edition, Duxbury Press, Pacific Grove.

be assigned to the option to delay a decision. That benefit should be considered a cost of taking immediate action versus the alternative of delaying that action pending more information. However, the burdens of delay—including any harm to public health, safety, and the environment—need to be analyzed carefully.

1. Quantitative Analysis of Uncertainty

Examples of quantitative analysis, broadly defined, would include formal estimates of the probabilities of environmental damage to soil or water, the possible loss of habitat, or risks to endangered species as well as probabilities of harm to human health and safety. There are also uncertainties associated with estimates of economic benefits and costs, such as the cost savings associated with increased energy efficiency. Thus, your analysis should include two fundamental components: a quantitative analysis characterizing the probabilities of the relevant outcomes and an assignment of economic value to the projected outcomes. It is essential that both parts be conceptually consistent. In particular, the quantitative analysis should be conducted in a way that permits it to be applied within a more general analytical framework, such as benefit-cost analysis. Similarly, the general framework needs to be flexible enough to incorporate the quantitative analysis without oversimplifying the results. For example, you should address explicitly the implications for benefits and costs of any probability distributions developed in your analysis.

As with other elements of regulatory analysis, you will need to balance thoroughness with the practical limits on your analytical capabilities. Your analysis does not have to be exhaustive, nor is it necessary to evaluate each alternative at every step. Attention should be devoted to first resolving or studying the uncertainties that have the largest potential effect on decision making. Many times these will be the largest sources of uncertainties. In the absence of adequate data, you will need to make assumptions. These should be clearly identified and consistent with the relevant science. Your analysis should provide sufficient information for decision makers to grasp the degree of scientific uncertainty and the robustness of estimated probabilities, benefits, and costs to changes in key assumptions.

For major rules involving annual economic effects of $1 billion or more, you should present a formal quantitative analysis of the relevant uncertainties about benefits and costs. In other words, you should try to provide some estimate of the probability distribution of regulatory benefits and costs. In summarizing the probability distributions, you should provide some estimates of the central tendency (e.g., mean and median) along with any other information you think will be useful such as ranges, variances, specified low-end and high-end percentile estimates, and other characteristics of the distribution.

Your estimates cannot be more precise than their most uncertain component. Thus, your analysis should report estimates in a way that reflects the degree of uncertainty and not create a false sense of precision. Worst-case or conservative analyses are not usually adequate because they do not convey the complete probability distribution of outcomes, and they do not permit calculation of an expected value of net benefits. In many health and safety rules, economists conducting benefit-cost analyses must rely on formal risk assessments that address a variety of risk management questions such as the baseline risk for the affected population, the safe level of exposure or, the amount of risk to be reduced by various interventions. Because the answers to some of these questions are directly used in benefits analyses, the risk assessment methodology must allow for the determination of expected benefits in order to be comparable to expected costs. This means that conservative assumptions and defaults (whether motivated by science policy or by precautionary instincts), will be incompatible with benefit analyses as they will result in benefit estimates that exceed the expected value. Whenever it is possible to characterize quantitatively the probability distributions, some estimates of expected value (e.g., mean and median) must be provided in addition to ranges, variances, specified low-end and high-end percentile estimates, and other characteristics of the distribution.

Whenever possible, you should use appropriate statistical techniques to determine a probability distribution of the relevant outcomes. For rules that exceed the $1 billion annual threshold, a formal quantitative analysis of uncertainty is required. For rules with annual benefits and/or costs in the range from 100 million to $1 billion, you should seek to use more rigorous approaches with higher consequence rules. This is especially the case where net benefits are close to zero. More rigorous uncertainty analysis may not be necessary for rules in this category if simpler techniques are sufficient to show robustness. You may consider the following analytical approaches that entail increasing levels of complexity:

- Disclose qualitatively the main uncertainties in each important input to the calculation of benefits and costs. These disclosures should address the uncertainties in the data as well as in the analytical results. However, major rules above the $1 billion annual threshold require a formal treatment.

- Use a numerical sensitivity analysis to examine how the results of your analysis vary with plausible changes in assumptions, choices of input data, and alternative analytical approaches. Sensitivity analysis is especially valuable when the information is lacking to carry out a formal probabilistic simulation. Sensitivity analysis can be used to find "switch points"—critical parameter values at which estimated net benefits change sign or the low cost alternative switches. Sensitivity analysis usually proceeds by changing one variable or assumption at a time, but it can also be done by varying a combination of variables simultaneously to learn more about the robustness of your results to widespread changes. Again, however, major rules above the $1 billion annual threshold require a formal treatment.

- Apply a formal probabilistic analysis of the relevant uncertainties, possibly using simulation models and/or expert judgment as revealed, for example, through Delphi methods.[*] Such a formal analytical approach is appropriate for complex rules where there are large, multiple uncertainties whose analysis

[*] The purpose of Delphi methods is to generate suitable information for decision making by eliciting expect judgment. The elicitation is conducted through a survey process which eliminates the interactions between experts. See Morgan MG and Henrion M (1990), *Uncertainty: A Guide to Dealing with Uncertainty in Quantitative Riskand Policy Analysis*, Cambridge University Press.

raises technical challenges, or where the effects cascade; it is required for rules that exceed the $1 billion annual threshold. For example, in the analysis of regulations addressing air pollution, there is uncertainty about the effects of the rule on future emissions, uncertainty about how the change in emissions will affect air quality, uncertainty about how changes in air quality will affect health, and finally uncertainty about the economic and social value of the change in health outcomes. In formal probabilistic assessments, expert solicitation is a useful way to fill key gaps in your ability to assess uncertainty.* In general, experts can be used to quantify the probability distributions of key parameters and relationships. These solicitations, combined with other sources of data, can be combined in Monte Carlo simulations to derive a probability distribution of benefits and costs. You should pay attention to correlated inputs. Often times, the standard defaults in Monte Carlo and other similar simulation packages assume independence across distributions. Failing to correctly account for correlated distributions of inputs can cause the resultant output uncertainty intervals to be too large, although in many cases the overall effect is ambiguous. You should make a special effort to portray the probabilistic results—in graphs and/or tables— clearly and meaningfully.

New methods may become available in the future. This document is not intended to discourage or inhibit their use, but rather to encourage and stimulate their development.

*Cooke RM (1991), *Experts in Uncertainty: Opinion and Subjective Probability in Science*, Oxford University Press.

2. Economic Values of Uncertain Outcomes

In developing benefit and cost estimates, you may find that there are probability distributions of values as well for each of the outcomes. Where this is the case, you will need to combine these probability distributions to provide estimated benefits and costs.

Where there is a distribution of outcomes, you will often find it useful to emphasize summary statistics or figures that can be readily understood and compared to achieve the broadest public understanding of your findings. It is a common practice to compare the "best estimates" of both benefits and costs with those of competing alternatives. These "best estimates" are usually the average or the expected value of benefits and costs. Emphasis on these expected values is appropriate as long as society is "risk neutral" with respect to the regulatory alternatives. While this may not always be the case, you should in general assume "risk neutrality" in your analysis. If you adopt a different assumption on risk preference, you should explain your reasons for doing so.

3. Alternative Assumptions

If benefit or cost estimates depend heavily on certain assumptions, you should make those assumptions explicit and carry out sensitivity analyses using plausible alternative assumptions. If the value of net benefits changes from positive to negative (or vice versa) or if the relative ranking of regulatory options changes with alternative plausible assumptions, you should conduct further analysis to determine which of the alternative assumptions is more appropriate. Because different estimation methods may have hidden assumptions, you should analyze estimation methods carefully to make any hidden assumptions explicit.

# NOTES

## EPIGRAPH

1 JOHN MAYNARD KEYNES, THE GENERAL THEORY OF EMPLOYMENT, INTEREST AND MONEY 113–14 (1936).

2 FRANK H. KNIGHT, RISK, UNCERTAINTY, AND PROFIT (1933).

3 OFF. OF MGMT. & BUDGET, EXEC. OFF. OF THE PRESIDENT, CIRCULAR NO. A-4, REGULATORY ANALYSIS 39 (2003), www.transportation.gov [hereinafter CIRCULAR A-4], included here as appendix B.

## INTRODUCTION

1 JOHN MAYNARD KEYNES, THE GENERAL THEORY OF EMPLOYMENT, INTEREST AND MONEY 113–14 (1936). A valuable discussion of neglect of catastrophic risks is Jonathan B. Wiener, *The Tragedy of the Uncommons: On the Politics of Apocalypse*, 7 GLOB. POL'Y 67 (2016).

## CHAPTER 1. WHAT WE DON'T KNOW

1 Henry A. Kissinger, *How the Enlightenment Ends*, ATLANTIC (June 2018), www.theatlantic.com.

2 For one view, see Nassim Nicholas Taleb et al., *The Precautionary Principle (with Application to the Genetic Modification of Organisms)* (Sept. 4, 2014) (unpublished manuscript), www.fooledbyrandomness.com; in particular, at 11:

   A lack of observations of explicit harm does not show absence of hidden risks. Current models of complex systems only contain the subset of reality that is accessible to the scientist. Nature is much richer than any model of it. To expose an entire system to something whose potential harm is not understood because extant models do not predict a negative outcome is not justifiable; the relevant variables may not have been adequately identified.

3 For the best treatment of the general problem, see WILLIAM D. NORDHAUS, THE CLIMATE CASINO (2015).

4 *Social Cost of Greenhouse Gases*, OFF. OF MGMT. & BUDGET, EXEC. OFF. OF THE PRESIDENT, https://obamawhitehouse. archives.gov (last visited June 27, 2020).

5 Robert S. Pindyck, *Fat Tails, Thin Tails, and Climate Change Policy*, 5 REV. ENV'T ECON. & POL'Y 258 (2010), available at http://web. mit.edu.

6 On that approach, see RICHARD L. REVESZ & MICHAEL A. LIVERMORE, REVIVING RATIONALITY (2020).

7 I am bracketing the various problems with cost-benefit analysis, including the priority of welfare and the relevance of distributional considerations. Superb treatments are REVESZ & LIVERMORE, *supra* note 6; MATTHEW ADLER, MEASURING SOCIAL WELFARE (2019). For my own discussion, see CASS R. SUNSTEIN, THE COST-BENEFIT REVOLUTION (2017).

8 Pindyck puts it this way: "If climate change turns out to be moderate, and its impact turns out to be moderate, we may not have too much to worry about. But what if climate change and its impact turn out to be catastrophic—the far right tail of the outcome distribution. It is that possibility, even if the probability is low, that might drive us to quickly adopt a stringent emission abatement policy. In effect, by reducing emissions now we would be buying insurance. But how much of a premium should we be willing to pay for such insurance? The answer depends in part on society's degree of risk aversion, which is complex and hard to evaluate." Robert S. Pindyck, *What We Know and Don't Know about Climate Change, and Implications for Policy* (NBER Working Paper No. 27304, 2019), available at www.nber.org.

9 *Cf.* Michael Greenstone & Vishan Nigam, *Does Social Distancing Matter?* (Univ. of Chi., Becker Friedman Inst. for Econ. Working Paper No. 2020–26, 2020), https://ssrn.com/abstract=3561244. Greenstone and Nigam do not, however, focus on the worst cases.

10 *See* Eric A. Posner & E. Glen Weyl, *Cost-Benefit Analysis of Financial Regulations: A Response to Criticisms*, 124 YALE L.J.F. 246 (2015).

11  Pindyck, *supra* note 5, at 270:

> Does buying insurance now against a catastrophic climate outcome make sense? It may or may not. As with any insurance policy, the answer depends on the cost of the insurance and the likelihood and impact of a catastrophe. The cost of the insurance might indeed be warranted if the probability of a catastrophe is sufficiently large and the likely impact is sufficiently catastrophic. But note that we don't need a fat-tailed probability distribution to determine that "climate insurance" is economically justified. All we need is a significant (and it can be small) probability of a catastrophe, combined with a large benefit from averting or reducing the impact of that catastrophic outcome.

12  An exceptionally clear discussion is William D. Nordhaus, *The Economics of Tail Events with an Application to Climate Change*, 5 REV. ENV'T ECON. & POL'Y 240 (2011).

13  Arden Rowell, *Regulating Best-Case Scenarios*, 50 ENV'T L. (forthcoming 2020), https://ssrn.com.

14  *See* ADLER, *supra* note 7.

15  This claim is meant to be less rigid than it sounds. It should be taken as a presumption rather than a rule. Distributive considerations or welfarist considerations might trump the cost-benefit analysis. *See* REVESZ & LIVERMORE, *supra* note 6; Matthew Adler, WELFARE AND FAIR DISTRIBUTION (2011). As discussed in the main text, there is also a legitimate role for risk aversion of certain kinds.

16  I am bracketing a possible *institutional* defense of the maximin principle, which is that it is a defense against some systematic bias on the part of regulators, such as undue optimism or short-term thinking. If regulators are systematically biased, the maximin principle might plausibly be a corrective.

### CHAPTER 2. WITH AND WITHOUT NUMBERS

1  Robert S. Pindyck, *What We Know and Don't Know about Climate Change, and Implications for Policy* (NBER Working Paper No. 27304, 2019), available at www.nber.org.

2  *See* TALI SHAROT, THE OPTIMISM BIAS (2011). On the behavioral findings discussed in this paragraph, *see* RICHARD THALER,

MISBEHAVING (2015); DANIEL KAHNEMAN, THINKING, FAST AND SLOW (2012); CASS R. SUNSTEIN, BEHAVIORAL SCIENCE AND PUBLIC POLICY (2021). On behavioral science and catastrophe, *see* Jonathan Wiener, *The Tragedy of the Uncommons: On the Politics of Apocalypse*, 7 GLOB. POL'Y 67 (2016).

3 For a vigorous defense of frequentism as the only plausible foundation of probability judgments, *see* JOHN KAY & MERVYN KING, RADICAL UNCERTAINTY: DECISION-MAKING BEYOND THE NUMBERS 57–68, 110–22 (2020). *See also* Gerd Gigerenzer, *How to Make Cognitive Illusions Disappear: Beyond "Heuristics and Biases,"* 2 EUR. REV. SOC. PSYCH. 83 (1991); Gerd Gigerenzer, *Why the Distinction between Single-Event Probabilities and Frequencies Is Important for Psychology (and Vice Versa)*, in SUBJECTIVE PROBABILITY 129, 129–61 (George Wright & Peter Ayton eds., 1994).

4 Eric-Jan Wagenmakers et al., *Bayesian versus Frequentist Inference*, in BAYESIAN EVALUATION OF INFORMATIVE HYPOTHESES 181 (Herbert Hoijtink et al. eds., 2008).

5 For a brisk, illuminating notation, see Daniel Kahneman & Amos Tversky, *On the Reality of Cognitive Illusions*, 103 PSYCH. REV. 582, 586 (1996):

> Whether or not it is meaningful to assign a definite numerical value to the probability of survival of a specific individual, we submit (a) that this individual is less likely to die within a week than to die within a year and (b) that most people regard the preceding statement as true—not as meaningless—and treat its negation as an error or a fallacy.

6 *See* KAY & KING, *supra* note 3, at 74–84.

7 *See id.*

8 Memorandum from John P. Holdren, Assistant to the President for Sci. & Tech. Dir., Off. of Sci. & Tech. Policy, Cass R. Sunstein, Admin., Off. of Info. & Regul. Affs., Off. of Mgmt. & Budget, & Islam A. Siddiqui, Chief Agric. Negotiator, U.S. Trade Representative, on Principles for Regulation and Oversight of Emerging Technologies to Heads of Executive Departments & Agencies (Mar. 11, 2011), https://obamawhitehouse.archives.gov, included here as appendix A.

9 *Id.*

10 *See* Improving Regulation and Regulatory Review, 3 C.F.R. § 13563 (2020).

11 *See* CIRCULAR A-4, appendix B. The relevant passage is worth quoting at length:

> Whenever possible, you should use appropriate statistical techniques to determine a probability distribution of the relevant outcomes. For rules that exceed the $1 billion annual threshold, a formal quantitative analysis of uncertainty is required. For rules with annual benefits and/or costs in the range from 100 million to $1 billion, you should seek to use more rigorous approaches with higher consequence rules. This is especially the case where net benefits are close to zero. More rigorous uncertainty analysis may not be necessary for rules in this category if simpler techniques are sufficient to show robustness.

12 OFF. OF INFO. & REGUL. AFFS., OFF. OF MGMT. & BUDGET, EXEC. OFF. OF THE PRESIDENT, 2015 REPORT TO CONGRESS ON THE BENEFITS AND COSTS OF FEDERAL REGULATIONS AND AGENCY COMPLIANCE WITH THE UNFUNDED MANDATES REFORM ACT 25 (2015), www.whitehouse.gov [hereinafter 2015 REPORT].

13 OFF. OF INFO. & REGUL. AFFS., OFF. OF MGMT. & BUDGET, EXEC. OFF. OF THE PRESIDENT, 2014 REPORT TO CONGRESS ON THE BENEFITS AND COSTS OF FEDERAL REGULATIONS AND UNFUNDED MANDATES ON STATE, LOCAL, AND TRIBAL ENTITIES 25 (2014), www.whitehouse.gov [hereinafter 2014 REPORT].

14 OFF. OF INFO. & REGUL. AFFS., OFF.OF MGMT. & BUDGET, EXEC. OFF. OF THE PRESIDENT, 2013 REPORT TO CONGRESS ON THE BENEFITS AND COSTS OF FEDERAL REGULATIONS AND UNFUNDED MANDATES ON STATE, LOCAL, AND TRIBAL ENTITIES 27 (2013), www.whitehouse.gov.

15 OFF. OF INFO. & REGUL. AFFS., OFF. OF MGMT. & BUDGET, EXEC. OFF. OF THE PRESIDENT, 2013 REPORT TO CONGRESS ON THE BENEFITS AND COSTS OF FEDERAL REGULATIONS AND UNFUNDED MANDATES ON STATE, LOCAL, AND TRIBAL ENTITIES 26 (2012), www.whitehouse.gov.

16 *See* 2015 REPORT, *supra* note 12, at 13–18.

17  *See id.* at 19.

18  *See id.* (food safety rules).

19  *See id.*

20  *See* 2014 REPORT, *supra* note 13.

21  As an analogy, consider the social cost of carbon, with a range, in 2020 dollars, from $12 to $123 per ton. INTERAGENCY WORKING GRP. ON SOC. COST OF GREENHOUSE GASES, U.S. GOV'T, TECHNICAL SUPPORT DOCUMENT: TECHNICAL UPDATE OF THE SOCIAL COST OF CARBON FOR REGULATORY IMPACT ANALYSIS UNDER EXECUTIVE ORDER 12866 (Aug. 2016), https://obamawhitehouse.archives.gov.

22  Arden Rowell, *Regulating Best-Case Scenarios*, 50 ENV'T L. (forthcoming 2020), https://ssrn.com.

23  *See* STEPHEN M. GARDNER, A PERFECT MORAL STORM: THE ETHICAL TRAGEDY OF CLIMATE CHANGE 411–14 (2011).

24  Broadly related arguments, emphasizing worst cases and low-probability risks of catastrophe, can be found in Martin L. Weitzman, *Fat Tails and the Social Cost of Carbon*, 104 AM. ECON. REV. 544 (2014); Martin L. Weitzman, *Fat-Tailed Uncertainty in the Economics of Catastrophic Climate Change*, 5 REV. ENV'T. ECON. & POL. 275 (2011); Martin L. Weitzman, *On Modeling and Interpreting the Economics of Catastrophic Climate Change*, 91 REV. ECON. & STAT. 1 (2009).

### CHAPTER 3. THE MAXIMIN PRINCIPLE

1  *See* JOHN KAY & MERVYN KING, RADICAL UNCERTAINTY: DECISION-MAKING BEYOND THE NUMBERS 114–16 (2020).

2  For a superb discussion, with many implications for policy, see ANNIE DUKE, THINKING IN BETS (2018). I should note that, for any gambler, the first bet must be made with an adequate bankroll, which means that a gambler would choose (a) only assuming that she had that. (Thanks to Annie Duke for this qualification.)

3  *See* Martin L. Weitzman, *Fat-Tailed Uncertainty in the Economics of Catastrophic Climate Change*, 5 REV. ENV'T. ECON. & POL. 275, 275 (2011); *see also* William D. Nordhaus, *The Economics of Tail Events with an Application to Climate Change*, 5 REV. ENV'T ECON. & POL'Y 240 (2011).

4  *See* Nordhaus, *supra* note 3.

5  *See* Robert S. Pindyck, *Fat Tails, Thin Tails, and Climate Change Policy*, 5 Rev. Env't Econ. & Pol'y 258 (2010), available at http://web.mit.edu.

6  *See* Nordhaus, *supra* note 3, at 241.

7  As Nordhaus puts it: "The basic proposition underlying the dismal theorem is that with 'fat-tailed' distributions, decision analyses may lead to very unintuitive results. This arises because distributions with fat tails are ones for which the probabilities of rare events decline relatively slowly as the event moves far away from its central tendency. This means that it can be hard to detect fat-tailed distributions and very hard to know how fat the tails are." *Id.* at 244.

8  *Id.*

9  Weitzman, *supra* note 3, at 275.

10  *See id.* at 285: "The result of this lengthy cascading of big uncertainties is a reduced form of truly extraordinary uncertainty about the aggregate welfare impacts of catastrophic climate change, which is represented mathematically by a PDF that is spread out and heavy with probability in the tails."

11  *See generally* Sendhil Mullainathan & Jann Spiess, *Machine Learning: An Applied Econometric Approach*, 31 J. Econ. Persp. 87 (2017).

12  Arden Rowell, *Regulating Best-Case Scenarios*, 50 Env't L. (forthcoming 2020), https://ssrn.com.

13  Michael Greenstone & Vishan Nigam, *Does Social Distancing Matter?* (Univ. of Chi., Becker Friedman Inst. for Econ. Working Paper No. 2020–26, 2020), https://ssrn.com.

## CHAPTER 4. THE PRECAUTIONARY PRINCIPLE

1  For general discussion, see Cass R. Sunstein, Laws of Fear (2006).

2  *See* Nassim Nicholas Taleb et al., *The Precautionary Principle (with Application to the Genetic Modification of Organisms)* (Sept. 4, 2014) (unpublished manuscript), www.fooledbyrandomness.com.

3  *Id.* Taleb et al. focus on "propagating impacts resulting in irreversible and widespread damage." In their understanding, the Precautionary Principle is designed "to avoid a certain class of what, in probability and insurance, is called 'ruin' problems. A ruin

problem is one where outcomes of risks have a non-zero probability of resulting in unrecoverable losses."

4 WINGSPREAD CONFERENCE ON THE PRECAUTIONARY PRINCIPLE, SCI. & ENV'T HEALTH NETWORK, THE WINGSPREAD STATEMENT ON THE PRECAUTIONARY PRINCIPLE (1998) (quoted in BJORN LOMBORG, THE SKEPTICAL ENVIRONMENTALIST 347 (2001)).

5 *See The Precautionary Principle*, RACHEL'S ENV'T & HEALTH WKLY., Feb. 18, 1998, www.rachel.org.

6 *See* Andrew Stirling, *Precaution in the Governance of Technology*, in OXFORD HANDBOOK OF LAW, REGULATION, AND TECHNOLOGY 645, 649 (Roger Brownsword et al. eds., 2017).

7 *See* SUNSTEIN, LAWS OF FEAR, *supra* note 1; JOHN GRAHAM & JONATHAN WIENER, RISK VS. RISK (1997). To that extent, it is not right to say that "criticism of the Precautionary Principle" is necessarily or generally rooted "on the overtly political grounds that it addresses general concerns like environment and human health, rather than more private interests like commercial profit or the fate of a particular kind of technology." Stirling, *supra* note, at 650. The "general concerns" may be on both sides.

8 *See* Cass R. Sunstein, *Health-Health Tradeoffs*, 63 U. CHI. L. REV. 1533 (1996).

9 *See* David Vogel, *The Regulation of GMOs in Europe and the United States: A Case-Study of Contemporary European Regulatory Politics* (Publication of the Study Group on Trade, Science and Genetically Modified Foods, 2001), www.cfr.org; *Are the US and Europe Heading for a Food Fight over Genetically Modified Food?*, PEW INITIATIVE FOOD & BIOTECHNOLOGY (Oct. 24, 2001), web.archive.org (archived from the original); Tony Gilland, *Precaution, GM Crops, and Farmland Birds*, in RETHINKING RISK AND THE PRECAUTIONARY PRINCIPLE 84, 84–88 (Julian Morris ed., 2001).

10 BILL LAMBRECHT, DINNER AT THE NEW GENE CAFE: HOW GENETIC ENGINEERING IS CHANGING WHAT WE EAT, HOW WE LIVE, AND THE GLOBAL POLITICS OF FOOD (2001) (tracing but not endorsing the various objections).

11 *Id.*

12 U.S. DEP'T OF TRANSP., PREPARING FOR THE FUTURE OF TRANSPORTATION: AUTOMATED VEHICLES 3.0 (AV 3.0) (2018), www.transportation.gov.

13 Teena Maddox, *How Autonomous Vehicles Could Save Over 350K Lives in the US and Millions Worldwide*, ZDNET (Feb. 1, 2018), www.zdnet.com.

14 *See* National Bioengineered Food Disclosure Standard, 83 Fed. Reg. 65,814, 65,869 (Dec. 21, 2018).

15 Note that the uncertainty is, by hypothesis, bounded; it is within specific ranges that probabilities cannot be assigned.

16 *See* National Bioengineered Food Disclosure Standard, *supra* note 14; Richard T. Woodward & Richard C. Bishop, *How to Decide When Experts Disagree: Uncertainty-Based Choice Rules in Environmental Policy*, 73 LAND ECON. 492 (1997).

17 *See* John C. Harsanyi, *Morality and the Theory of Rational Behavior*, in UTILITARIANISM AND BEYOND 40 (Amartya Sen & Bernard Williams eds., 1982).

18 *See* Cass R. Sunstein, *Probability Neglect: Emotions, Worst Cases, and Law*, 112 YALE L.J. 61, 62–63 (2002).

19 *See* Todd S. Aagaard, *A Functional Approach to Risks and Uncertainties under NEPA*, 1 MICH. J. ENV'T & ADMIN. L. 87 (2012).

20 *See* Richard A. Musgrave, *Maximin, Uncertainty, and the Leisure Trade-Off*, 88 Q.J. ECON. 625, 626–28 (1974).

21 CIRCULAR A-4, Appendix B. A useful primer can be found at OFF. OF INFO. & REGUL. AFFS, OFF. OF MGMT. & BUDGET, EXEC. OFF. OF THE PRESIDENT, REGULATORY IMPACT ANALYSIS: A PRIMER, www.reginfo.gov (last visited May 30, 2020).

22 CIRCULAR A-4, *appendix B*.

23 *Id.*

24 *Id.*

25 *See* JOHN KAY & MERVYN KING, RADICAL UNCERTAINTY: DECISION-MAKING BEYOND THE NUMBERS (2020).

26 William D. Nordhaus, *The Economics of Tail Events with an Application to Climate Change*, 5 REV. ENV'T ECON. & POL'Y 240, 256 (2011).

27 *See* RICHARD H. THALER, *The Psychology of Choice and the Assumptions of Economics*, in QUASI RATIONAL ECONOMICS 137, 143 (1991) (arguing that "losses loom larger than gains"); Daniel Kahneman, Jack L. Knetsch & Richard H. Thaler, *Experimental Tests of the Endowment Effect and the Coase Theorem*, 98 J. POL. ECON. 1325, 1328 (1990); Colin Camerer, *Individual Decision Making*, in THE HANDBOOK OF EXPERIMENTAL ECONOMICS, 587, 665–70 (John H. Kagel & Alvin E. Roth eds., 1995).

28 Deborah A. Kermer et al., *Loss Aversion Is an Affective Forecasting Error*, 17 PSYCH. SCI. 649 (2006).

29 *See* William Samuelson & Richard Zeckhauser, *Status Quo Bias in Decision Making*, 1 J. RISK & UNCERTAINTY 7 (1988).

30 *See* PAUL SLOVIC, THE PERCEPTION OF RISK 140–43 (2000).

31 *See* Daniel B. Botkin, *Adjusting Law to Nature's Discordant Harmonies*, 7 DUKE ENV'T L. & POL'Y F. 25, 27 (1996).

32 *Id.*

33 *Id.* at 33.

34 *See* Sydney E. Scott & Paul Rozin, *Actually, Natural Is Neutral*, 4 NATURE HUM. BEHAV. 989 (2020). For a valuable discussion, see ARDEN ROWELL & KENWORTHY BILZ, THE PSYCHOLOGY OF ENVIRONMENTAL LAW (2021).

### CHAPTER 5. UNCERTAINTY

1 FRANK H. KNIGHT, RISK, UNCERTAINTY, AND PROFIT (1933); KIYOHIKO G. NISHIMURA & HIROYUKI OZAKI, ECONOMICS OF PESSIMISM AND OPTIMISM: THEORY OF KNIGHTIAN UNCERTAINTY AND ITS APPLICATIONS (2017).

2 On ignorance and precaution, see Poul Harremoes, *Ethical Aspects of Scientific Incertitude in Environmental Analysis and Decision Making*, 11 J. CLEANER PROD. 705 (2003).

3 *See* Nassim Nicholas Taleb et al., *The Precautionary Principle (with Application to the Genetic Modification of Organisms)* (Sept. 4, 2014) (unpublished manuscript), www.fooledbyrandomness.com.

4 *See* CIRCULAR A-4, *appendix B.*

5 *Id.*

6 *See* Cass R. Sunstein, *The Limits of Quantification*, 102 CALIF. L. REV. 1369 (2014).

7 *See* JOHN RAWLS, A THEORY OF JUSTICE 146 (revised ed. 1999) ("When we have no evidence at all, the possible cases are stipulated to be equally probable."); R. DUNCAN LUCE & HOWARD RAIFFA, GAMES AND DECISIONS 284 (1957).

8 *See* Cass R. Sunstein, *Irreversible and Catastrophic*, 91 CORNELL L. REV. 841 (2006).

9 *See* JOHN KAY & MERVYN KING, RADICAL UNCERTAINTY: DECISION-MAKING BEYOND THE NUMBERS 63–64 (2020).

10 For a technical treatment of the possible rationality of maximin, see Kenneth J. Arrow & Leonid Hurwicz, *An Optimality Criterion for Decision-Making under Ignorance*, in UNCERTAINTY AND EXPECTATION IN ECONOMICS 1 (C. F. Carter & J. L. Ford eds., 1972); for a nontechnical overview, *see* JON ELSTER, EXPLAINING TECHNICAL CHANGE 185–207 (1983).

11 Taleb et al., *supra* note 3.

12 *See* ELSTER, *supra* note 10, at 188–205.

13 *See, e.g., id.*

14 *See* Rawls, *supra* note 7, at 132–39. Rawls draws on but adapts WILLIAM FELLNER, PROBABILITY AND PROFIT 140–42 (1965).

15 Rawls, *supra* note 7, at 134.

16 *Id.*

17 *Id.*

18 I am cheating a little bit here, referring to the original rather than the revised version of Rawls's book. *See* JOHN RAWLS, A THEORY OF JUSTICE 155 (1971). (Sometimes the original is best.) It should be noted that, in later work in particular, Rawls emphasized the Kantian foundations of the veil of ignorance—*see* JOHN RAWLS, POLITICAL LIBERALISM (1993)—and that those ideas could also be connected with the difference principle. I am bracketing that possibility for my purposes here.

19 RAWLS, THEORY OF JUSTICE (1971), *supra* note 18.

20 *Id.* (Note: This is only in the original, again.)

21 I am grateful to Annie Duke for this point.

22 *See* Stephen Gardiner, *The Core Precautionary Principle*, 14 J. POL. PHIL. 33 (2006).

23 *Id.* at 46.

24 *Id.* at 49.

25  *Id.* at 51.

26  *Id.* at 55.

27  *See id.* at 51–52.

28  *See id.* at 55.

29  *See* ELSTER, *supra* note 10, at 203.

30  *See* Robert S. Pindyck, *Fat Tails, Thin Tails, and Climate Change Policy*, 5 REV. ENV'T ECON. & POL'Y 258, 260 (2010), available at http://web.mit.edu.

31  Taleb et al., *supra* note 3.

## CHAPTER 6. OBJECTIONS

1  *Cf.* David Kelsey, *Choice under Partial Uncertainty*, 34 INT'L ECON. REV. 297, 305 (1993):

> It is often argued that lexicographic decision rules such as maximin are irrational, since in economics we would not expect an individual to be prepared to make a small improvement in one of his objectives at the expense of large sacrifices in all of his other objectives. This criticism is less powerful in the current context since we have assumed that the decision maker has a weak order rather than a cardinal utility function on the space of outcomes. Given this assumption the terms "large" and "small" used in the above argument are not meaningful.
>
> In many contexts, however, decision makers do have a cardinal utility function, not merely a weak order.

2  *See* WILLIAM D. NORDHAUS & JOSEPH BOYER, WARMING THE WORLD: ECONOMIC MODELS OF CLIMATE CHANGE 168 (2000).

3  *See* Kym Anderson & Chantal Pohl Nielsen, *Golden Rice and the Looming GMO Debate: Implications for the Poor* 7–8 (Ctr. for Econ. Pol'y Rsch., Discussion Paper No. 4195, 2004), https://ssrn.com.

4  *See* Richard T. Woodward & Richard C. Bishop, *How to Decide When Experts Disagree: Uncertainty-Based Choice Rules in Environmental Policy*, 73 LAND ECON. 492 (1997).

5  *See, e.g.*, Kenneth J. Arrow, *Some Ordinalist-Utilitarian Notes on Rawls's Theory of Justice*, 70 J. PHIL. 245 (1973); John C. Harsanyi, *Can the Maximin Principle Serve as a Basis for Morality? A Critique of John Rawls's Theory*, 69 AM. POL. SCI. REV. 594 (1975).

6  Richard A. Musgrave, *Maximin, Uncertainty, and the Leisure Trade-Off*, 88 Q.J. ECON. 625, 627 (1974).

7  *See* C. Y. Cyrus Chu & Wen-Fang Liu, *A Dynamic Characterization of Rawls's Maximin Principle: Theory and Implications*, 12 CONST. POL. ECON. 255, 268 (2001).

8  For an account and a lament, see JOHN KAY & MERVYN KING, RADICAL UNCERTAINTY: DECISION-MAKING BEYOND THE NUMBERS 106–54 (2020).

9  *See* MILTON FRIEDMAN, PRICE THEORY 282 (1976); *see also* JACK HIRSHLEIFER & JOHN G. RILEY, THE ANALYTICS OF UNCERTAINTY AND INFORMATION 10 (1992):

> In this book we disregard Knight's distinction, which has proved to be a sterile one. For our purposes risk and uncertainty mean the same thing. It does not matter, we contend, whether an "objective" classification is or is not possible. For, we will be dealing throughout with a "subjective" probability concept (as developed especially by Savage, 1954): probability is simply *degree of belief*. . . . [Because we never know true objective probabilities, d]ecision-makers are . . . never in Knight's world of risk but instead always in his world of uncertainty. That the alternative approach, assigning probabilities on the basis of subjective degree of belief, is a workable and fruitful procedure will be shown constructively throughout this book.

> For the purposes of the analysis by Hirshleifer and Riley, the assignment of subjective probabilities may well be the best approach. But the distinction between risk and uncertainty is not sterile when regulators are considering what to do but lack information about the probabilities associated with various outcomes.

10  *See* DECISION MAKING UNDER DEEP UNCERTAINTY (Vincent Marchau et al. eds., 2019). Stephen F. LeRoy & Larry D. Singell, Jr., *Knight on Risk and Uncertainty*, 95 J. POL. ECON. 394 (1987). For a vigorous and sustained argument on behalf of the pervasiveness of uncertainty, see KAY & KING, *supra* note 8, at 35–49. For a clear explanation of why uncertainty exists, see JON ELSTER, EXPLAINING TECHNICAL CHANGE 193–99 (1983). ("One could certainly elicit from a political scientist the subjective probability

that he attaches to the prediction that Norway in the year 3000 will be a democracy rather than a dictatorship, but would anyone even contemplate *acting* on the basis of this numerical magnitude?").

11 *See* ELSTER, *supra* note 10.

12 *Id.*

13 For a good overview of this topic, see JONATHAN BARON, THINKING AND DECIDING 125–47 (3d ed. 2000). Elster briefly notes how this point relates to the debate over uncertainty: "There are too many well-known mechanisms that distort our judgment, from wishful thinking to rigid cognitive structures, for us to be able to attach much weight to the numerical magnitudes that can be elicited by the standard method of asking subjects to choose between hypothetical options." ELSTER, *supra* note 10, at 199 (internal citations omitted).

14 *See* Amos Tversky & Daniel Kahneman, *Judgment under Uncertainty: Heuristics and Biases*, in JUDGMENT UNDER UNCERTAINTY: HEURISTICS AND BIASES 3, 11 (Daniel Kahneman ed., 1982); Timur Kuran & Cass R. Sunstein, *Availability Cascades and Risk Regulation*, 51 STAN. L. REV. 683 (1999).

15 *See* ELSTER, *supra* note 10, at 199.

16 JOHN MAYNARD KEYNES, A TREATISE ON PROBABILITY 214 (1921).

17 *Id.*

18 I am bracketing here frequentist claims about the pervasiveness of uncertainty. *See* KAY & KING, *supra* note 8, at 35–49. Even if we are frequentists, regulators are often dealing with repeated cases for which frequentist assignments of probability are perfectly feasible— consider food safety, occupational safety, and air pollution.

19 *But see generally* KAY & KING, *supra* note 8.

20 On some of the complexities here, see CASS R. SUNSTEIN, THE COST-BENEFIT REVOLUTION (2018).

## CHAPTER 7. IRREVERSIBILITY

1 *See generally* Benoit Morel et al., *Pesticide Resistance, the Precautionary Principle, and the Regulation of Bt Corn: Real Option and Rational Option Approaches to Decisionmaking*, in BATTLING RESISTANCE TO ANTIBIOTICS AND PESTICIDES 184 (Ramanan

Laxminarayan ed., 2003) (proposing option theory as an analytical framework for the Precautionary Principle and applying that framework to the issue of commercializing Bt corn); Justus Wesseler, *Resistance Economics of Transgenic Crops under Uncertainty: A Real Options Approach*, in *id.* at 214 (discussing pest resistance as an irreversible cost of transgenic crops).

2  *See* Indur M. Goklany, THE PRECAUTIONARY PRINCIPLE: A CRITICAL APPRAISAL OF ENVIRONMENTAL RISK ASSESSMENT 6 (2001).

3  Quoted in BJORN LOMBORG, THE SKEPTICAL ENVIRONMENTALIST 347 (2001).

4  *See* SAN FRANCISCO PRECAUTIONARY PRINCIPLE ORDINANCE, available at http://temp.sfgov.org.

5  42 U.S.C. § 102 (c)(5).

6  *See* Metcalf v. Daley, 214 F.3d 1135, 1143 (9th Cir. 2000); Scientists' Inst. for Pub. Info. v. Atomic Energy Comm'n, 481 F.2d 1079, 1090–91 (D.C. Cir. 1973); Sierra Club v. Marsh, 769 F.2d 868, 879 (1st Cir. 1985).

7  *See, e.g.*, 33 U.S.C. § 2712(j) (making special exception to planning requirements for the use of federal resources in situations requiring action to "avoid irreversible loss of natural resources"); 42 U.S.C. § 9611(i) (same exception for Superfund cleanups); 22 U.S.C. § 2151p-1(c)(2)(A) (requiring the president to assist developing countries in a way that responds to "the irreversible losses associated with forest destruction").

8  *See* Sierra Club v. Marsh, 872 F.2d 497, 499–500 (1st Cir. 1989); on the complexities here, see the discussion in the section "Seriousness and Sunk Costs," below.

9  *See* David A. Dana, *Existence Value and Federal Preservation Regulation*, 28 HARV. ENVTL. L. REV. 343, 345 (2004); Charles J. Cicchetti & Louis J. Wilde, *Uniqueness, Irreversibility, and the Theory of Nonuse Values*, AM. J. AGRIC. ECON. 1121, 1121–22 (1992).

10  *See* Ohio v. U.S. Dep't of the Interior, 880 F.2d 432, 464 (D.C. Cir. 1989).

11  Cicchetti & Wilde, *supra* note 9, at 1122 (noting Weisbrod's analogy of such amenities to public goods, in that "individuals who may never purchase the commodity still hold a value for the option to do

so"). The independent use of option value is, however, challenged in various places. *See, e.g.*, A. MYRICK FREEMAN III, JOSEPH A. HERRIGES & CATHERINE L. KLING, THE MEASUREMENT OF ENVIRONMENTAL AND RESOURCE VALUES 249–51 (2003) (suggesting that "what has been called an option value is really just the algebraic difference between the expected values of two different points on a WTP [willingness to pay] locus").

12 *See* Ohio, 880 F.2d at 464.

13 *See, e.g.*, Determination of Critical Habitat for the Mexican Spotted Owl, 60 Fed. Reg. 29,914, 29,928 (June 6, 1995); 43 C.F.R. § 11.83. *But see* 69 Fed. Reg. 68,444, 68,514 n.51 (Nov. 24, 2004) (doubting whether option value should be recognized as separate from other values).

14 *See* FRANK ACKERMAN & LISA HEINZERLING, PRICELESS: ON KNOWING THE PRICE OF EVERYTHING AND THE VALUE OF NOTHING 185 (2004).

15 For a helpful overview, see Richard C. Bishop, *Option Value: An Exposition and Extension*, 58 LAND ECON. 1 (1982).

16 *See* TOM COPELAND & VLADIMIR ANTIKAROV, REAL OPTION 8–13 (2001).

17 *See* RICHARD BREALEY & STEWART MYERS, PRINCIPLES OF CORPORATE FINANCE 565 (2002).

18 *Id.* at 582.

19 COPELAND & ANTIKAROV, *supra* note 16, at 13.

20 *See generally* CASS R. SUNSTEIN, ONE CASE AT A TIME (1999).

21 Bradley C. Karkkainen, *Toward a Smarter NEPA: Monitoring and Managing Government's Environmental Performance*, 102 COLUM. L. REV. 903 (2002).

22 *See* Kenneth Arrow & Anthony C. Fisher, *Environmental Preservation, Uncertainty and Irreversibility*, 88 Q.J. ECON. 312, 313–14 (1974).

23 *Id.* at 319.

24 *See* ANTHONY C. FISHER, UNCERTAINTY, IRREVERSIBILITY, AND THE TIMING OF CLIMATE POLICY 9 (2001), available at http://are.berkeley.edu.

25 I use the word "uncertain" to refer to both risk and uncertainty. "Risk" exists when it is possible to assign probabilities to various

outcomes; "uncertainty" exists when no probabilities can be assigned. For the seminal discussion, which has prompted a heated debate, see FRANK H. KNIGHT, RISK, UNCERTAINTY, AND PROFIT (1933). For a nontechnical overview, see JON ELSTER, EXPLAINING TECHNICAL CHANGE (1983).

26 *See* RICHARD A. POSNER, CATASTROPHE 161–62 (2004). A more technical discussion to the same effect is contained in Graciela Chichilnisky & Geoffrey Heal, *Global Environmental Risks*, 7 J. ECON. PERSPS. 65, 76 (1993), emphasizing the need for a distinctive approach to "risks that are poorly understood, endogenous, collective, and irreversible." *Id.* at 67. For a more detailed treatment of option value and irreversibility, see *id.* at 76–84.

27 POSNER, *supra* note 26, at 161–62.

28 *Id.* at 162.

29 *See* Chichilnisky & Heal, *supra* note 26, at 76.

30 For a useful treatment, see Neil A. Manson, *The Concept of Irreversibility: Its Use in the Sustainable Development and Precautionary Principle Literatures*, 1 ELEC. J. SUSTAINABLE DEV. 1 (2007).

31 On this idea in the environmental context, see Sierra Club v. Marsh, 872 F.2d 497 (1st Cir. 1989); Leslye A. Herrmann, Comment, *Injunctions for NEPA Violations: Balancing the Equities*, 59 U. CHI. L. REV. 1263 (1992).

32 *See* AVINASH DIXIT & ROBERT PINDYCK, INVESTMENT UNDER UNCERTAINTY 6 (1994) ("When a firm makes an irreversible investment expenditure, it exercises, or 'kills,' its option to invest. It gives up the possibility of waiting for new information to arrive that might affect the desirability or timing of the expenditure, and this lost option value is an opportunity cost that must be included as part of the investment.").

33 *Id.* at 6.

34 Robert S. Pindyck, *What We Know and Don't Know about Climate Change, and Implications for Policy* (NBER Working Paper No. 27304, 2019), available at www.nber.org.

35 *Id.*

36 FISHER, *supra* note 24, at 11.

37 *See* POSNER, *supra* note 26.

38  Pindyck, *supra* note 34.
39  Good discussions can be found in ELIZABETH ANDERSON, VALUE IN ETHICS AND ECONOMICS (1993); JOSEPH RAZ, THE MORALITY OF FREEDOM (1985).
40  Remarks of Vernon L. Smith, in GLOBAL CRISIS, GLOBAL SOLUTIONS 627 (Bjorn Lomborg ed., 2004).
41  *See generally* Juan Almendares, *Science, Human Rights, and the Precautionary Principle in Honduras*, in PRECAUTION, ENVIRONMENTAL SCIENCE, AND PREVENTIVE PUBLIC POLICY 55 (Joel A. Tickner ed., 2003) (discussing advantages to Third World countries offered by the Precautionary Principle).

## CONCLUSION

1  *See, e.g.*, Kenneth J. Arrow & Leonid Hurwicz, *An Optimality Criterion for Decision-Making Under Uncertainty*, in UNCERTAINTY AND EXPECTATION IN ECONOMICS 1 (C. F. Carter & J. L. Ford eds., 1972) (suggesting the rationality of either maximin or maximax).
2  *See* John C. Harsanyi, *Morality and the Theory of Rational Behavior, in* UTILITARIANISM AND BEYOND (Amartya Sen & Bernard Williams eds., 1982).
3  *See, e.g.*, R. Duncan Luce & Howard Raiffa, Games and Decisions 286–97 (1957).
4  William D. Nordhaus, *The Economics of Tail Events with an Application to Climate Change*, 5 REV. ENV'T ECON. & POL'Y 240, 247 (2011). Importantly, Nordhaus adds, at 250:
    The applicability of the dismal theorem depends upon some very restrictive assumptions. First, it is necessary that the probability distribution of consumption has a sufficiently fat tail so that tail events become quantitatively important. Second, it is necessary that risk aversion be sufficiently powerful that these tail events have a significant impact on the overall utility. And under both of these assumptions, the distribution must go to the limit of catastrophe and not have a finite bound or upper or lower limit.
    Note as well the importance of considering the costs of indulging in high levels of risk aversion. As noted in the text, "sufficiently

powerful" risk aversion will give rise not only to high known costs
but also to serious, and possibly catastrophic, risks.

5  *Cf.* Robert S. Pindyck, *Fat Tails, Thin Tails, and Climate Change
Policy*, 5 REV. ENV'T ECON. & POL'Y 258, 272–73 (2010): "But as
with any insurance policy, what matters for climate insurance is the
cost of the insurance (in this case the cost of abatement) and its
expected benefit, in terms of how it will shift the distribution for
possible outcomes. . . . The case for climate insurance is made more
complicated (and harder to justify) by the fact that we face other
potential catastrophes that could have impacts of magnitudes that
are similar to those of a climate catastrophe. If catastrophes—climate
or otherwise—would each reduce GDP and consumption by a
substantial amount, then they cannot be treated independently. That
is, potential nonclimate catastrophes will affect the WTP to avert or
reduce a climate catastrophe and affect the economics of 'climate
insurance.'"

6  NORMAN FROHLICH & JOE A. OPPENHEIMER, CHOOSING
JUSTICE: AN EXPERIMENTAL APPROACH TO ETHICAL
THEORY (1992).

7  *Id.*

8  Some of this material is drawn from the current version of
CIRCULAR A-4. *See* appendix B.

9  *See* Arden Rowell, *Regulating Best-Case Scenarios*, 50 ENV'T L.
(forthcoming 2020), https://ssrn.com. Rowell's illuminating
discussion refers to "wonders."

10  *See* RICHARD L. REVESZ & MICHAEL A. LIVERMORE,
REVIVING RATIONALITY (2020).

11  *See id.*; MATTHEW ADLER, MEASURING SOCIAL WELFARE
(2019), on "prioritarianism."

12  Pindyck, *supra* note 5, at 273.

# INDEX

Page numbers in *italics* indicate tables.

aggressive regulation, 39
aggressive responses, to COVID-19 pandemic, 39, 107–8, 116
air pollution, 103; irreversible, 93; regulations, 24–25, 41, 51
animals, uncertainty of, 76
Arrow, Kenneth, 90
artificial intelligence, 7, 36
atmospheric GHG concentrations, 8, 17, 91, 98
autonomous vehicles, 45, 57, 110
availability bias, 77
availability heuristic, 10, 17, 77
average utility, 112
avoidance strategies, 62–64, 68

Bayesian approaches: costs and benefits assessed in, 53; of frequentists, 61–62; to probability judgments, 21–22
benefits and costs. *See* costs and benefits
Benthamite calculations, 3, 5, 78–79
best-case scenarios, 25–26, 66, 109–10, 115
Bin Laden, Osama, 52–53
bounded uncertainty, 79

breakeven analysis, 40–41, 63, 108, 114

calculations, judgments versus, 15
carbon, social cost of, 1, 7
carbon tax, 81
catastrophe, 9; distributional considerations, 80–81; irreversibility and, 83; miracles in averting, 2; probabilities in cost-benefit analysis, 12, 32; uncertain dangers of, 72–74
catastrophe-miracle tradeoffs, 26–27, 37, 58
catastrophic harm, 61, 70–71, 74–75, 101
Catastrophic Harm Precautionary Principle, 64, 74–75, 95
catastrophic hazards, 111–12
catastrophic outcomes: from climate change, 32–33, 35, 53–54, 69, 97, 116–17; of COVID-19 pandemic, 116
catastrophic risks, 8–10, 17, 27, 32; of climate change, 36, 91; low-probability, 34; maximin principle on, 81

Circular A-4, OMB, 24, 50–52, 63, 113–14, 127–36, 141n11

climate change: catastrophic outcomes from, 32–33, 35, 53–54, 69, 97, 116–17; catastrophic risks of, 36, 91; fat tails in probability distributions, 34–35; irreversibility of, 82–87, 91, 93–95, 97–99, 113; maximin principle for, 72–73; pandemics, emerging technologies and, 23, 26–27, 71; Pindyck on, 7–8, 16–17, 61, 116–17, 138n8; policy, 1, 8; probability distributions for outcomes, 16–17, 117; RCPP on, 69; regulations for, 91, 104; uncertainties of, 7–8, 16–17, 61; valuation of damage from, 86; "wait and learn" approach to, 99, 103, 107

climate insurance, 117, 138n8, 139n11, 155n5

conservationists, 98

coordination of federal agencies, in approach to emerging technologies, 123–24

coronavirus. See COVID-19 pandemic of 2020

cost-benefit analysis: aggressive regulation and, 39; expected values in, 11, 111; limited information in, 23; maximin principle and, 108, 110; in Office of Information and Regulatory Affairs reports, 24; in Principles for Regulation and Oversight of Emerging Technologies, 22–23; probabilities and, 45; probabilities of catastrophic events and, 12, 32; probability distribution and, 33; quantitative, 9; of "wait and learn" approach toward climate change, 99; worst-case scenarios and, 11

costs and benefits: in Bayesian decision, 53; breakeven analysis of, 40–41; of emerging technologies, 123; monetized, 25, 45, 63; of non-environmental-related health and safety rules, 25–26, 26; of possible outcomes, 10; probability distributions and, 13; of regulations, 22–25, 45, 52, 63

Council of Environmental Quality, 48

COVID-19 pandemic of 2020, 11, 16, 28; aggressive responses to, 39, 107–8, 116; catastrophic outcomes, 116; information gaps in decisions, 107; losses from, 82; risk aversion toward, 115; risks and, 18–19; stay-at-home mandate, 73; uncertainties in, 61; vaccine for, 55

danger: of catastrophe, uncertain, 72–74; maximin principle and, 46–50; uncertain, 62–63, 72–74

data gathering and analysis, in regulatory decisions, 63

decision theory, 2, 42

difference principle, 112

distributional goals, irreversible harms and, 103–4

doctors, assigning probabilities, 18–21

economic values, of uncertain outcomes, 134

Elster, Jon, 70, 78, 150n13

emerging technologies, 23, 26–27, 36, 51, 71, 122–25

Emerging Technologies Interagency Policy Coordination Committee (ETIPC), 121–22

emissions. *See* greenhouse gas emissions

endangered species, 100–101, 103

environmental goods, monetary valuation of, 86–88

environmental harm, 43–44, 74, 84, 93, 99–100

environmental impact statements, 84, 89

environmental law and statutes, on irreversibility, 83–84, 89

environmental preservation, 90

environmental protections and regulations, 90–92, 95, 97, 101–2, 105

environmental risks, 80, 95–96

epistemic limits, 23–24

ETIPC. *See* Emerging Technologies Interagency Policy Coordination Committee

Executive Order 13563, 121–22, 124

existence value, option value and, 86–89

expected value, 29–32, 38; in cost-benefit analysis, 11, 111; human welfare and, 115–16; maximin principle and, 35; maximizing, 52; negative, 37; of options, policymakers on, 10

exponential growth neglect, 18

extreme outcomes, 33–35, 70

fair distribution, 13

fairness, regulations and, 80–81

familiar and unfamiliar risks, 56

fat tails: maximin principle for problems involving, 12, 70, 108–9; in probability distributions, 32–35, 70, 143n7

federal regulation, 1

financial crisis, 11, 14

Fisher, Anthony, 90, 97

flexibility: with emerging technologies, 123; future, preserving, 85, 87–89, 91–92, 99, 102, 104, 113; "wait and learn" approach and, 103

Food and Drug Administration, 55

formal probabilistic analysis, of uncertainties, 51, 133

frequentists, 21–22, 61–62, 79

Friedman, Milton, 75

future flexibility, maintaining and preserving, 85, 87–89, 91–92, 99, 102, 104, 113

future generations, 85, 98, 101–3

Gardiner, Stephen, 67–70, 72–73, 109, 116

genetically modified foods, 7, 70–71, 73; catastrophic risks of, 91; regulation of, 43–45; risks from, 56, 64–65, 91, 104

GHG emissions. *See* greenhouse gas emissions

Great Depression, 2–3

greenhouse gas (GHG) emissions, 1–2, 16, 69, 72–73; atmospheric concentrations of, 8, 17, 91, 98; capital costs of reducing, 97–99, 103; cumulative effect of, 98–99; irreversible effects of, 84–85, 91, 98–99; reductions, 70, 97–99, 103

harm: catastrophic, 61, 70–71, 74–75, 101; Catastrophic Harm Precautionary Principle, 64, 74–75, 95; environmental, 43–44, 74, 84, 93, 99–100; irreparable, 95; irreversible, 84, 87, 91, 95–97, 103–4; Irreversible Harm Precautionary Principle, 83–84, 87, 90, 92–93, 95–97, 99, 101–5

Harsanyi, John, 47–49, 112

health-health tradeoffs, 44, 107–8

health risks, 18–21, 44

ignorance, 40; maximin principle and, 13–15; regulators in conditions of, 62

imperfect knowledge, 90–92

inaction, option of, 37–38

incommensurability, irreversibility and, 100–102

infinite risk aversion, 74–75

information gaps and limits, 23, 50–51, 107

international cooperation, for emerging technologies, 125

investments, irreversible, 96

irrationality, maximin principle and, 47–48

irreparable harm, 95

irreversibility: catastrophe and, 83; of climate change and environmental damage, 82–87, 91, 93–95, 97–99, 113; distribution, least well-off and, 103–4; environmental law and statutes on, 83–84, 89; of GHG emissions and reductions, 84–85, 91, 98–99; incommensurability and, 100–102; interpretations and characterizations of, 92–94; optimal delay and, 102–3; Precautionary Principle on, 83–86; regulations and, 85, 87, 90, 96–97; seriousness of, 94–95; sunk costs and, 92–93, 96–97, 99; uncertainty and, 90–92, 97

irreversible harm, 84, 87, 91, 95–97, 103–4

Irreversible Harm Precautionary Principle, 83–84, 87, 90, 92–93, 95–97, 99; on diverse social goods, 102; on losses, 101; qualifications, 102–5

irreversible losses, 82, 85, 87, 151n7; from climate change, 113; environmental statutes on, 84, 89; from GHG reductions, 98–99; of species, 100; tradeoffs for, 101

judgments: calculations versus, 15; probability, 21–22, 77–78
judicial minimalism, 88–89
justice, Rawls on, 65–66

Kay, John, 52–53
Kelsey, David, 148n1
Keynes, John Maynard, 2–5, 12, 17, 61, 78–79
King, Mervyn, 52–53
Knight, Frank, 76, 149n9
Knightian uncertainty, 11–12, 23–24, 39; maximin principle and, 108–9; probabilities and, 13–14, 19, 21–22, 65; regulators in situations of, 62
knowledge: of climate change, irreversibility and, 84–85; gaps in, 22–27, 35–36; imperfect, 90–92; uncertain, 3–5, 78

the least well-off, distribution of irreversibilities and, 103–4
loss aversion, 54–59
low-probability, high-magnitude risks, 36

machine learning, 36
margin of safety, 10–11
maximax principle, 66
maximin principle: on catastrophic hazards, 111–12; on catastrophic risks, 81; for climate change, 72–73; cost-benefit analysis and, 108, 110; danger and, 46–50; expected values and, 35; Harsanyi's criticism of, 47–49;

ignorance and, 13–15; irrationality or madness produced by, 47–48; Knightian uncertainty and, 108–9; for new technologies, 115; for options with two possible outcomes, 67; for problems involving fat tails, 12, 70, 108–9; for problems involving monetary gambles, 28–42; Rawls on, 65–67, 72–74, 109, 112; RCPP and, 68–69; for regulation and regulators, 8–9, 11–12, 29–30, 52, 64, 72–73, 81, 109–10, 139n16; in regulatory policy, 8–9, 67, 71, 75, 79–80; risk aversion and, 49–50; risks and, 8, 27, 49, 112; uncertainty and, 65, 72–79, 108–10, 112; on worst-case scenarios, 8–9, 14, 19–20, 35, 44, 47–50, 64–66, 109–10, 112–15
maximin principle, objections to: distributional considerations, 80–81; infinite risk aversion, 74–75; regulatory problems involving uncertainty are not usual, 79–80; triviality of argument, 72–74; uncertainty does not exist, 75–79
Memorandum for the Heads of Executive Departments and Agencies (2011), 22–23, 121–25
miracles, 2; catastrophe-miracle tradeoffs, 26–27, 37, 58; new technologies and, 26–27; potential returns from, 37; regulations and, 12–13, 26, 58, 115

monetary gambles, maximin principle for problems involving, 28–42

monetary valuation, of environmental goods, 86–88

monetized costs and benefits, 25, 45, 63

Monte Carlo simulations, 51, 134

mortality risks, 42, 48

mythical benevolence of nature, 58–60

narratives, in regulations, 52–53

National Environmental Policy Act (NEPA) of 1970, 84, 89, 99

nature, mythical benevolence of, 58–60

negative expected value, 37

NEPA. See National Environmental Policy Act of 1970

new technologies, 30, 36, 57–59; miracles and, 26–27; monetized costs and benefits of, 63; risks from, 115

nonregulation, 27, 39, 44–45

Nordhaus, William D., 33–34, 53–54, 108–9, 143n7, 154n4

nuclear power, 70

Obama, Barack, 1, 52–53

objective probabilities, 76–78, 149n9

objective uncertainty, 75

OMB Circular A-4, 24, 50–52, 63, 113–14, 127–36, 141n11

optimal delay, irreversibilities and, 102–3

options, 10, 67; imperfect knowledge, precautions and, 90–92; inaction, 37–38; irreversibility and, 96

option theory, 88

option value, 86–91

the original position, justice and, 66

pandemics, 7, 12, 14, 18–19; climate change, emerging technologies and, 23, 26–27, 71; risky technologies and, 34; worst-case scenarios in, 73. See also COVID-19 pandemic of 2020

Paris Agreement, 16

personal probability, 75

Pindyck, Robert, 12; on climate change, 7–8, 16–17, 61, 116–17, 138n8; on climate insurance, 117, 138n8, 139n11, 155n5; on GHG reductions, 70, 98

policymakers: on costs and benefits of possible outcomes, 10; on expected value of options, 10; on fat tails in probability distributions, 33; uncertainties and, 16–17. See also regulatory policy

Posner, Richard, 91, 97–98

Precautionary Principle, 9, 144n7; Catastrophic Harm, 64, 74–75, 95; on environmental harm, 43–44; for environmental protections, 105; Gardiner on, 67; on genetically modified crops, 70; on irreversibility, 83–86;

Irreversible Harm, 83–84, 87, 90, 92–93, 95–97, 99, 101–5; loss aversion and, 55–57; mythical benevolence of nature and, 58–60; RCPP, 68–69, 116; regulations and, 44–45, 58; on risks, 43–44, 48

precautions: irreversibility of climate change and, 93–95; options, imperfect knowledge and, 90–92

precommitment value, 104–5

present bias, 17

preservation, environmental, 90

Principle of Insufficient Reason, 64

Principles for Regulation and Oversight of Emerging Technologies, White House, 2011 memorandum on, 22–23, 121–25

probabilities: assigning, 18–22; assigning to outcomes, 68–70, 109–11; of catastrophic events, in cost-benefit analysis, 12, 32; of catastrophic harm, 70–71; of catastrophic outcomes, 116; of catastrophic risks, 34; choices and decisions in, 75–76; in climate change policy, uncertainties and, 8; cost-benefit analysis and, 12, 32, 45; doctors on, 18–20; of extreme outcomes, 33–35; frequentists on, 21–22, 61–62, 79; of imaginable outcomes, 3, 11–12; Knightian uncertainty and, 13–14, 19, 21–22, 65; objective, 76–78, 149n9; personal, 75;

of potential outcomes, expected value and, 10; Principle of Insufficient Reason on, 64; risk aversion and, 48, 75; risks and, 61–62; subjective, 75–79, 149n9; uncertainties and, 76–77; unknown, 66–67, 116–17; of worst-case scenarios, 9, 11, 47–48, 64–65

probability distributions, 8, 10, 13, 24–25; for climate change outcomes, 16–17, 117; cost-benefit analysis and, 33; fat tails in, 32–35, 70, 143n7; OMB Circular A-4 on, 50–51

probability judgments, 21–22, 77–78

public participation, emerging technologies and, 122

public policy: maximin principle in, 8–9, 67; risk aversion in, 31

quantitative analysis: cost-benefit, 9; of uncertainty, 50–51, 130–34

Rawls, John, 65–68, 72–74, 80, 109, 112

Rawlsian Core Precautionary Principle (RCPP), 68–69, 116

regulations, 7; aggressive, 39; air pollution, 24–25, 41, 51; of autonomous vehicles, 45, 110; breakeven analysis in, 41; catastrophic risk and, 27; climate change, 91, 104; costs and benefits of, 22–25, 45, 52, 63;

regulations (*cont.*)
data gathering and analysis in decisions, 63; distributional matters in, 80–81; of emerging technologies, 124–25; environmental protections and, 90–92, 95, 97, 101–2; fairness and, 80–81; of genetically modified foods, 43–45; ignorance of regulators and, 62; irreversibility and, 85, 87, 90, 96–97; maximin principle and, 8–9, 11–12, 29–30, 52, 64, 72–73, 81, 109–10, 139n16; miracles and, 12–13, 26, 58, 115; narratives in, 52–53; nonregulation and, 27, 39, 44–45; on option value, in environmental context, 87; possibility of wonder and miracles and, 12–13; Precautionary Principle and, 43–45, 58; probability judgments and, 77–78; risk and, 23, 44, 55; uncertainty and, 23, 62, 109; worst-case scenarios and, 11, 25, 47, 54, 113–15

regulatory policy: decision theory and, 2; maximin principle in, 8–9, 67, 71, 75, 79–80; OMB Circular A-4 on uncertainty in, 127–34; RCPP in, 68; on worst-case scenarios, 47, 54

resilience and robustness, in handling uncertain risks, 53

Rio Declaration, 1992, 43, 83

risk assessment and risk management, for emerging technologies, 123

risk aversion, 10–11, 13, 29–30, 35–36, 154n4; to catastrophic harms, 74–75; fat-tailed problems and, 108–9; infinite, 74–75; maximin principle and, 49–50; probabilities and, 48, 75; in public policy, 31; toward COVID-19 pandemic, 115; on welfare grounds, 49

risk-risk tradeoffs, 44–46

risks: catastrophic, 8–10, 17, 27, 32, 34, 36, 81, 91; Catastrophic Harm Precautionary Principle on, 64; COVID-19 pandemic and, 18–19; environmental, 80, 95–96; familiar and unfamiliar, 56; from genetically modified foods, 56, 64–65, 91, 104; health, 18–21, 44; limited information and, 23; loss aversion and, 55–56; low-probability, high-magnitude, 36; maximin principle and, 8, 27, 49, 112; mortality, 42, 48; from new technologies, 115; of pandemic, 18; Precautionary Principle on, 43–44, 48; probability and, 61–62; probability judgments of, 77–78; regulation and, 23, 44, 55; uncertain, 53, 62–63; uncertainties and, 75, 78, 152n25

safety-safety tradeoffs, 45
Savage, L. J., 75, 77
Schelling, Thomas, 102–3
scientific integrity, emerging technologies and, 122

scientific uncertainty, 25, 50, 83
seriousness, sunk costs and, 92–99
social cost of carbon, 1, 7
social welfare, maximizing, 13
status quo, 38–39, 54–55, 57–59, 92
stay-at-home mandate, COVID-19 pandemic, 73
strategies of avoidance, 62–64
subjective probabilities, 75–79, 149n9
sunk costs: irreversibility and, 92–93, 96–97, 99; seriousness and, 92–99

Taleb, Nassim Nicholas, 70–71, 137n2, 143n3
technologies, 7; emerging, 23, 26–27, 36, 51, 71, 122–25; new, 26–27, 30, 36, 57–59, 63, 115; risky, 34
terrorist attacks, 14
tobacco smoking, annual deaths from, 59–60
tradeoffs: catastrophe-miracle, 26–27, 37, 58; health-health, 44, 107–8; irreversible losses and, 101; risk-risk, 44–46; safety-safety, 45; uncertainty-uncertainty, 45–46
triviality, of argument for maximin principle, 72–74

unavailability bias, 77–78
uncertain dangers, 62–63; of catastrophe, 72–74
uncertain knowledge, 3–5, 78
uncertain risks, 53, 62–63

uncertainty: of animals, 76; bounded, 79; breakeven analysis for, 63; of climate change, 7–8, 16–17, 61; in climate change policy, 8; in COVID-19 pandemic, 61; extreme outcomes and, 35; formal probabilistic analysis of, 51, 133; formal quantitative analysis of, 50–51; irreversibility and, 90–92, 97; Knightian, 11–14, 19, 21–24, 39, 62, 65, 108–9; maximin principle and existence of, 75–79; maximin principle on, 65, 72–74, 108–10, 112; objective, 75; OMB Circular A-4 on, 63; OMB Circular A-4 on quantitative analysis of, 130–34; OMB Circular A-4 on treatment of, 127–30; probability and, 76–77; regulation and, 23, 62, 109; in regulatory problems, as not usual, 79–80; risks and, 75, 78, 152n25; scientific, 25, 50, 83
uncertainty-uncertainty tradeoffs, 45–46
United Nations Framework Convention on Climate Change, 83
unknown probability, 66–67, 116–17
unknown unknowns, 34–36

vaccine, COVID-19, 55
valuation of environmental goods, monetary, 86–88

value: economic, of uncertain outcomes, 134; existence, 86–89; expected, 10–11, 29–32, 35, 37–38, 52, 111; precommitment, 104–5; of uncertain outcomes, economic, 135

"wait and learn" approach, 99, 103, 107, 117
Weitzman, Martin, 32, 34–35
welfare, 30–31, 37–38, 49, 115–16
Wingspread Declaration, 43
World War II, 2–3

worst-case scenarios: best-case scenarios and, 25–26, 109–10; catastrophic, 32; cost-benefit analysis and, 11; maximin principle on, 8–9, 14, 19–20, 35, 44, 47–50, 64–66, 70, 109–10, 112–15; in pandemics, 73; probabilities of, 9, 11, 47–48, 64–65; public officials on, 13; in RCPP, 68; regulations and regulators on, 11, 25, 47, 54, 113–15; as threats to poorest people, 80–81

# ABOUT THE AUTHOR

Cass R. Sunstein is currently the Robert Walmsley University sity Professor at Harvard. He is Founder and Director of the Program on Behavioral Economics and Public Policy at Harvard Law School. In 2018, he received the Holberg Prize from the government of Norway, sometimes described as the equivalent of the Nobel Prize for law and the humanities. From 2009 to 2012, he was Administrator of the White House Office of Information and Regulatory Affairs; after that, he served on the President's Review Board on Intelligence and Communications Technologies and on the Pentagon's Defense Innovation Board. Mr. Sunstein has testified before congressional committees on many subjects, and he has advised officials at the United Nations, the European Commission, the World Bank, and many nations on issues of law and public policy. He serves as an adviser to the World Health Organization and the Behavioural Insights Team in the United Kingdom. Mr. Sunstein is author of hundreds of articles and dozens of books, including *Nudge: Improving Decisions about Health, Wealth, and Happiness* (with Richard H. Thaler, 2008), *Conformity* (2019), *How Change Happens* (2019), and *Too Much Information* (2020).